COMPARATIVE CONSTITUTIONAL ENGINEERING

Also by Giovanni Sartori

A TEORIA DE REPRESENTACAO NO ESTADO
  REPRESENTATIVO MODERNO
LA COMPARAZIONE NELLE SCIENZE SOCIALI
  (*editor with Leonardo Morlino*)
CORRENTI, FRAZIONI E FAZIONE NEI PARTITI
  POLITICI ITALIANI (*editor*)
DEMOCRATIC THEORY
DEMOCRAZIA E DEFINIZIONI
ELEMENTI DI TEORIA POLITICA
EUROCOMMUNISM: The Italian Case (*editor with Austin Ranney*)
IL PARLAMENTO ITALIANO 1946–1963 (*editor*)
PARTIES AND PARTY SYSTEMS: A Framework for Analysis
LA POLITICA: Logica e Metodo in Scienze Sociali
SECONDA REPUBBLICA? SI, MA BENE
SOCIAL SCIENCE CONCEPTS: A Systematic Analysis (*editor*)
STATO E POLITICA NEL PENSIERO DI BENEDETTO
  CROCE
TEORIA DEI PARTITI E CASO ITALIANO
THE THEORY OF DEMOCRACY REVISITED
TOWER OF BABEL: On the Definition and Analysis of Concepts
  in the Social Sciences (*with F. W. Riggs and H. Teune*)

Comparative Constitutional Engineering

An Inquiry into Structures, Incentives and Outcomes

Giovanni Sartori
Albert Schweitzer Professor in the Humanities
Columbia University

 NEW YORK UNIVERSITY PRESS
Washington Square, New York

First published in the U.S.A. in 1994 by
NEW YORK UNIVERSITY PRESS
Washington Square
New York, N.Y. 10003

Library of Congress Cataloging-in-Publication Data
Sartori, Giovanni, 1924–
[Seconda Repubblica?   English]
Comparative constitutional engineering : an inquiry into structures,
incentives and outcomes / Giovanni Sartori.
p.   cm.
Includes bibliographical references and index.
ISBN 0–8147–7974–3
1. Italy—Politics and government—1976–   2. Italy—Politics and
government—1945–1976.   I. Title.
JN5451.S2713   1994
320.445—dc20   94–26676
                                                                    CIP

Printed in Great Britain

Contents

Preface

The proper study of politics is not man but institutions.

John Plamenatz

Bentham once said that the two great 'engines' of reality are punishment and reward. And, to be sure, 'engineering' is a derivative of engine. Putting metaphor and etymology together I come up with 'constitutional engineering' as a title that conveys, first, that constitutions are like (somewhat like) engines, i.e., mechanisms that must 'work' and that must have an output of sorts; and, second, that constitutions are unlikely to work as intended unless they employ the engines of Bentham, i.e., punishments and rewards. Indeed, in much of this book I argue the case for conceiving and building constitutions as incentive-based structures.

The title also indicates that the book is comparative. Indeed, it is 'very comparative'. The general idea is that by comparing we draw lessons from other countries. Right. However, and further, this work is 'systematically comparative' both in coverage and in method. In coverage because the arguments are drawn from, and extend to, all existing democratic forms; and in method because the analysis crucially relies on comparative control: all generalizations are checked *vis-à-vis* the cases to which they apply.

The work is divided into three parts, namely, (i) Electoral Systems, (ii) Presidentialism and Parliamentarism, and (iii) Issues and Proposals. Electoral systems may not be formally included in the constitutional text and yet remain, in fact, a most essential part of the workings of political systems. Not only are electoral systems the most manipulative instrument of politics; they also shape the party system and affect the spectrum of representation. They are thus reviewed first. I overview proportional representation systems, the single member district system, and the various (little known or unduly neglected) double ballot formulas. Which are, in each case, the effects of any given system? It will be shown that the literature on electoral systems is often quite wrong in its causal analysis and also in its praises and blames. The Lijphart thesis that proportional representation is always better in that it is conducive to consensus democracy is untenable; the 'direct-ness' of single member district systems is often dubious and must be related to 'localism'; the double ballot systems need not be majoritarian but can also apply to multi-member (if small) electoral districts.

Part Two provides an underpinning of presidential versus semi-presidential systems. I propose definitions of both, single out the borderline cases (such as Finland), and then probe the conditions that indeed 'condition' the performance of presi-dentialism and semi-presidentialism. Why does South-Amer-ican presidentialism seldom work? And under what conditions does the American prototype work best? Assuming that undivided government is the major working condition of presidential systems, one must also consider party discipline (or, conversely, its lack) in Congress, the degree of opinion polarization, and other factors. As for French-type semi-presidentialism, the major asset of its dual authority structure appears to be that the formula can cope with divided government.

Part Two also discusses in detail the parliamentary systems – largely a misnomer for a variety of fundamentally different formulas. The English system clearly is a premiership system; the German *Kanzlerdemokratie* is a controlled parliamentary system; whereas at the other end one finds assembly systems (the French III and IV Republic) whose working capabilities hinge on party discipline, on the degree to which parliaments are party-controlled. Here again, condition analysis is crucial. The English system hinges on a single-member district system which does produce single party government (a condition that fails to apply to India). The German formula presupposes a two-and-a-half party system, and can hardly be successfully extended and even less exported to four-five party systems.

The Third Part illustrates – among other things – a new proposal, namely, a system of alternating or intermittent presidentialism that squarely confronts the straits of both the hopeless presidential systems (for instance, Brazil) and of the non-working parliamentary systems (for instance, Italy and Israel). The proposal may also be usefully considered for Mexico and for Eastern, post-communist countries (especially Poland and Russia). At bottom the problem is to combine effective parliamentary control with efficient government. Whether power is divided (as in pure presidentialism), or shared, in either case Western-type polities easily stumble in stalemate, paralysis and inefficiency. I thus propose and illustrate a legislative process for adverse conditions that neither allows parliamentary obstructionism nor, at the other extreme, the kind of government by decree to which Latin American presidentialism is dangerously prone.

As the relatively modest size of the book shows by itself, this is a quick-paced work – partly by design, and partly because the pace of events has quickened. When I embarked upon writing it, I did not plan an erudite work but an eminently practice-oriented signalling of what was wrong, or was wrongly understood, about democratic political structures. At the time – it was about the end of 1991 – my sense was that after some fifty years of political freezing we were entering a 'change cycle', a time of impetuous change. But I did not myself expect the pace of institutional change to be as fast and as extended as it has become, across the world, in the last two years. And the quickness of events has somewhat forced me to close and present this work as quickly as possible. For the more I asked myself – along my drafting – whether we knew *how to change*, and what it was that demanded change, the more I discovered (to my own dismay) that the answer to that question was a resounding No, and that our 'reform happenings' bear the stamp of highly incompetent reformers. Maybe this is too harsh a judgment. Even so the question still is: In institutional matters do we know what to reform, how?

Columbia University GIOVANNI SARTORI
1 January 1994

Part One
Electoral Systems

1 Majoritarian and Proportional Systems

1.1 PREMISES

In the beginning is how a people is made to vote. Electoral systems determine how votes are translated into seats,[1] and thereby affect the behavior of the voter. They also bear on whether the elector votes party or persons. On the first account the criterion is whether the translation of votes into seats is 'in proportion' or not, and the major divide among electoral systems thus is between proportional and majoritarian representation. On the second account the criterion is who controls the selection of the candidates, and the major divide is between 'person voting' or not. Since both criteria admit degrees and mixes, the overall classification and typology of electoral systems turns out to be – unsurprisingly – an intricate matter.

Before entering the intricacies let us firm up the basics. In majoritarian systems the winner takes all; in proportional systems winning is shared and simply requires a sufficient share (generally the electoral quotient). In majoritarian systems the voter's choice is funnelled and ultimately narrowed into one alternative; in proportional systems voters are not forced into concentrating their vote and their range of choice may be quite extensive. On the other hand, majoritarian systems propose individual candidates, persons; proportional systems generally propose party lists. But each system admits a great deal of variation.

While all majoritarian systems are 'winner take all', the majority in question can either be an absolute majority (of at least 50.01 percent), or a relative majority, a plurality, i.e., the highest vote. On the other hand, while all proportional systems are required to translate votes into seats in 'some proportion', this proportion ranges from a quasi-perfect correspondence to a highly imperfect, i.e., highly disproportional one. Further, it

3

is not the case that all electoral systems can be classified as being either majoritarian or proportional. The double ballot system can either be a majoritarian system with single-member constituencies, or a proportional system with multi-member constituencies.

However, the real difficulty of dividing all electoral systems into either plurality or proportional resides in the fact that the two labels are not symmetric. When we say plurality we denote only an electoral criterion (the first wins all), while 'proportional representation' is also inevitably suggestive of a proportional outcome: a representative body that somehow reflects the vote distributions 'in proportion'. True, we always issue the warning that proportional representation may turn out to be highly disrepresentative. Even so, whenever a system is called proportional we assume that there must be a somewhat even ratio between votes and seats.

In order to tidy up the argument we must separate, I suggest, the criterion or method of electing from its outcome, that is, from how a parliament reflects the voting distributions of its electors. If so, majoritarian and proportional systems can be neatly identified and defined by reciprocal exclusion, as negatives of each other. To wit, an electoral system is majoritarian if the voting occurs in constituencies (usually single-member ones) in which the winner takes all: the so-called first-past-the-post system. Conversely, any electoral system in which the voting occurs in two-or-more member constituencies and produces two-or-more winners elected on a 'highest votes' basis, is a proportional system. To be sure, there are two very different ways of establishing these winning proportions: one (the most frequent one) is to determine electoral quotients; the other is to elect the front runners as they come (the first two in a two-member constituency, and so forth). In the first case candidates are elected on the basis of *equal shares* (quotients); in the second, candidates are elected on the basis of the *highest portions* of votes.

The doubt immediately arises as to whether quotients and rank-orderings can be assimilated as being both proportional criteria. I submit that they can, on the consideration that both produce proportional outcomes, and that each of the two criteria can deliver, *per se*, a same degree of fair proportionality.

The distinction that I have just proposed between majority and proportional systems does not imply that all electoral systems can be classified dichotomously as either being majoritarian or not, for we must also make allowance for 'mixed systems'. It must be immediately noted, however, that this notion is often misapplied. For instance, if we have a bicameral parliament whose lower and upper Houses are elected with different systems, this does not add up to being a mixed system. Truly mixed electoral systems are only the ones that elect a same chamber by combining proportional and plurality criteria.[2] But it is obvious that this hybrid does not undermine our divide and indeed presupposes it.[3]

1.2 MAJORITY SYSTEMS

Majority or majoritarian systems do not seek a parliament that reflects the voting distributions; they seek a clear winner. Their intent is not only to elect a parliament but at the same time to elect (if only by implication) a government. As already noted, the major difference among majoritarian systems lies in whether they require a relative majority, a plurality, or an absolute majority. In both cases we generally have single-member constituencies; in both cases we have, therefore, one winner that takes all; but a plurality winner simply is one who first passes the post and therefore, often, an expression of the *largest minority*, whereas an absolute majority winner does represent a true (above 50 percent) majority.

English-type majority systems are one-shot plurality systems. If an absolute majority winner is required, then one must have recourse to i) the alternative vote employed, e.g., in Australia for the Lower House, or ii) to the double ballot system that admits to the run-off only the two front runners of the first ballot.

The *alternative vote* (ATV) is a 'preferential' voting system within single-member districts that requires every elector to number all the candidates in order of preference.[4] The candidates with fewest first preferences are eliminated and preferences are redistributed until an absolute majority winner emerges. The alternative vote thus is a truly majoritarian system; it also permits and encourages – by strongly personalizing the vote – the crossing of party lines. As for the double ballot systems (to be taken up later), it is self-evident that if only two candidates are admitted to the second ballot one of them will be an absolute majority winner.

1.3   THE MAJORITY PREMIUM

Are there additional majoritarian systems? One might answer yes with reference to the majority premium, whose intent is indeed to fabricate or reinforce a majority. To be sure, the majority premium assumes proportional voting. Even so, the question as to where premiums stand *vis-à-vis* proportional representation deserves asking.

At one end we find, e.g., the Saenz Peña system applied in Argentina until 1962 which allocates, on a constituency basis, two-thirds of the seats to the list with the highest vote and the remaining one-third to the list with the second highest vote. There is little question that – aside from the anomaly of performing with list voting in multi-member constituencies – the Saenz Peña system fabricates a crushing absolute majority and comes as close to imposing a two-party constituency format as any arrangement conceivably can. But take, next, the formula that has long been adopted in the past in Paraguay: two-thirds of the seats to the party with the highest vote, and the remaining one-third distributed in proportion to all the other party lists. In spite of a still crushing premium, in this case one-third of the arrangement is proportional. Assume now that the premium does not allocate two-thirds of the seats but only a modest majority of, say, 55 percent. In this instance the crucial difference is whether the premium goes to a single plurality winner, or whether it goes to party electoral alliances (technically called *apparentement*: e.g., France in 1951 and 1956,

Italy in 1953). In the first hypothesis the analogy with a majoritarian system is still strong; but in the second hypothesis it is apparent that we have a proportional contest implemented by a bonus. However, if the premium requires the *apparentement*, the parties in alliance, to attain an absolute majority, then it simply reinforces an existing majority. If, instead, the premium can also go to less than 50 percent winners, then it fabricates a majority. But in both cases the fragmentation of the party system may largely remain as it is, and thus coalition governments remain the standing practice.

It is clear that the premium device finds little justification with three to four relevant parties (the systems that I call of limited pluralism) and applies best to fragmented party systems and when it compels parties to forge electoral alliances. Indeed, its purpose is not merely to ensure a majority but also to encourage aggregative processes. This is so because parties that fight an election in alliance can hardly vie with each other adversarially, and because the electoral alliance is assumed to be carried over into a governmental alliance, and thus into coalition governments. The nicety of this aggregative pressure is that – unlike the aggregative pressure brought about by the plurality system – it is based on interest and convenience.

But there is a hitch. The merits of the arrangement can be easily circumvented by parties that join forces simply in order to win a bonus, and that revert to their previous divisiveness as soon as the election is over. This eventuality can be discouraged, however, by stipulating that the premium is forfeited for all the parties that have benefitted from it, if and when their governmental coalition breaks down. The chances of a coalescent and cohesive coalitional behavior crucially depend on this clause.

1.4   PR SYSTEMS

Let us turn to proportional representation (PR for short). As already mentioned, while all PR systems purport to translate votes into seats in proportion, still they vary quite extensively in their respective degrees of proportionality or disproportionality. And it is wrong to assume that the proportionality of PR is established *only* by the translation formulas of votes into seats; it is equally and more decisively determined by the constituency size.

Starting with the translation formulas, with the seat allocation rules, the purest system of all is the *single transferable vote* (STV) in multi-member districts: the voters are required to number the candidates in order of preference; any vote surplus to the quota (the electoral quotient) is reassigned in accord to second preferences; and then the bottom candidates are successively eliminated and their preferences redistributed until all the seats are filled.

As we move from STV to less pure proportional systems, the better-known ones are (i) the method of 'largest remainder', (ii) the D'Hondt or 'highest average' method, and (iii) the Sainte-Laguë formula. The *largest remainder* system (e.g., Italy for the House of Deputies until 1993) favors the smaller parties. After one seat is assigned for any full quota (established by dividing votes by seats), any remaining seats are attributed to the parties with the largest residues or remainders. The *highest average* (D'Hondt) method is the most frequently used PR system (Austria, Belgium, Finland, Italy until 1993 for the Senate, and a number of Latin American countries) and is less proportional in that it favors the larger parties. Finally, the *Sainte-Laguë* method, used (in a modified version) only in Sweden and Norway, is less proportional than the largest remainder system but more proportional than the highest average method.[5]

The differences between the aforesaid systems are, we might say, mathematical. But the major factor in establishing the proportionality or disproportionality of PR is the *size of the constituency* – where 'size' is measured by the number of members that each district elects. So, and regardless of the mathematical fine points, the larger the constituency, the greater the proportionality.[6] Since the Netherlands and Israel perform as a nation-wide constituency (electing respectively 150 and 120 members), these two countries come closest to pure proportionality.[7] Conversely, the smaller the constituency, the lesser the proportionality. Thus countries with very small (from 2- to 5-member districts) or small-medium (up, say, to a maximum of 9–10-member districts) constituencies, are for this very reason countries of least-proportional proportionality.[8]

The caveat is, here, that this least-proportional proportionality may not show up in our measures, and this for the very simple reason that poor proportionality penalizes the smaller parties and eventually wipes them out. In this instance the disproportionality is revealed, then, by a small-sized party system which contains, e.g., only three or four parties. Awaiting the technical explanation of the point (*infra* 3.3 and 3.4), its logic is that the smaller the constituency, the greater the waste of votes, that is, of the below-quotient or below-winning votes that are simply lost. To be sure, the foregoing assumes that several parties enter the contest and that the matter ends at the district level. If a national list pools all the wasted constituency votes, and if the national quotient somehow corresponds to an average of the constituency quotas, then proportionality is restored (especially if the number of parliamentary seats is allowed to vary: the so-called additional member system).[9]

PR systems require multi-member districts. It is also generally the case that PR systems are list systems that confront the voter with party lists of names (often as many names as the number of members elected by any given district). These party lists can be (i) 'closed', meaning that the candidates are elected in the order determined by the party (e.g., Israel and most Latin American countries); (ii) 'open', meaning that there is no predetermined rank ordering and that the voters are allowed to express one or more preferences, ticking names on the list.[10] *Switzerland*

Aside from list voting, two other possible formulas are the 'free list' and the 'limited vote'. In the *free list* system the voter has as many votes as there are candidates to be elected; he or she can cumulate two votes on any one candidate, and is also permitted to cast a vote for candidates of different parties. The only significant application of all these freedoms is, however, in

Switzerland, where the government is prearranged in tenure and composition and is quite insensitive to whatever the free list system might produce. Finally, the *limited vote* gives each voter more than one vote, but fewer votes than members to be elected: for instance, in a three-member district voters are given two votes. We shall discuss this system in the next chapter.

The problem with majoritarian systems is that they are too manipulative. The problem with proportional systems is that they permit too many parties. This is less the case, to be sure, with impure proportionality. Thus imperfectly proportional PR finds its justification in being a means for countering the fragmentation of the party system. However, another – and concurrent – way of obstructing party proliferation is denial of access, that is, to establish thresholds for admission to representation. The German term for this device is *Sperrklausel*, barrier clause; and the German threshold has been set, from the outset, at the 5 percent level.[11] The device has been adopted by a number of countries, but the actual thresholds vary. At one extreme Israel had a perfectly useless threshold of 1 percent (raised to 1.5 in 1992); at the other extreme we find Turkey, with a 10 percent exclusion (in the 1983–1991 elections), and especially Greece, which has displayed, throughout its highly volatile electoral history, a series of above-15 percent barriers (interpreted as 'reinforced PR').[12] In the middle between these extremes – but on the low side – Spain has adopted a 4 percent and Argentina a 3 percent level of admission (or, conversely, of exclusion).

It is impossible to establish *a priori* and in general which is the right threshold, for its 'rightness' hinges in each country on what the distributions are. Certainly, going below a 3–4 percent level makes little sense, while a 10 percent threshold appears a pretty high hurdle. But a 5 percent exclusion would have been quite useless in Poland in 1991 and very effective in Italy in 1993. Be that as it may, exclusion barriers generally do serve the purpose for which they are intended. On the other hand, their effectiveness is being overblown in the German case – for it was not the *Sperrklausel* that eliminated neo-Nazism and the Communist party.

1.5   THE DOUBLE BALLOT

I have already pointed out that the double ballot system is very much a system by itself. For one, it allows voters to vote twice, with an interval of one or two weeks between the first vote and the run-off, and this implies that voters can knowingly reorient their choices on the basis of the returns of the first round. This is a very distinctive and, to my mind, a very important characteristic. On the other hand, the double ballot is a highly flexible system that allows for both majoritarian and proportional arrangements. The double ballot system is majoritarian with single-member constituencies, and proportional with multi-member constituencies.

Note, however, that it never is quite majoritarian-like nor fully proportional. It never is majoritarian-like in the sense that it does not have the coercive impact on the voter that characterizes the first-past-the-post system. Actually, in the first round voters perform as with proportional representation: they freely express their first preference for all the options.[13] Conversely, the double ballot is never adequately proportional, for its purpose would be defied by large multi-member constituencies. The double ballot makes little sense with larger than three- and at most four-member constituencies; and, as we know, the proportional performance of small districts is disproportional.

On these premises let us first take up the majoritarian version of the double ballot. The French Fifth Republic employs the double ballot both for its Presidential and parliamentary elections.[14] In the first case the requirement is, wisely, the absolute majority. Therefore for the presidential race only the first two front runners are admitted to the run-off. For the chamber of deputies the run-off requires only a plurality winner; and much depends on how many candidates are admitted to the second round. At the outset the admittance threshold was at 6 percent; but it has been gradually raised to 12.5 percent. We shall see later (*infra* 4.3) why the threshold matters, and therefore in what way the performance of the double ballot hinges on how many candidates are permitted to enter the second ballot. At the moment let us simply close on the note that, in the overall, the formula of the Fifth Republic has well served – since 1958 – the purpose of strongly reducing the fragmentation of the party system and of reshaping the French polity in a bipolar mold.[15]

There is no current instance, instead, of a double ballot system with, say, three-member constituencies (a formula that was employed, however, in the past). The purpose of this arrangement clearly is to give better chances to third parties or to minority parties. To be sure, under this formula the reductive effect (on the number of parties) of the system is lessened. On the other hand, since it is unwarranted to assume that every polity is best served by a two-party-like format, the proportional variety of the double ballot should be kept in mind. Note that in this instance no gate-keeping, no barrier, is necessary, for even if all the candidates are admitted to the run-off, the hopelessly outdistanced ones will either withdraw or wither away on their own.

Just one additional point. While the majoritarian second ballot does not require, at the first round, recourse to party lists (voters can be offered from the outset concrete candidates), the proportional variety of the second ballot does call for party lists, and preferably for open lists. In the end, however, both routes lead to a same outcome: e.g., in a three-member constituency the three candidates with the highest personal votes will be elected regardless of party.

NOTES

1. As a rule, parliamentary seats. Presidential elections, and any election to non-divisible office, require a separate evaluation.
2. The current instances of such mixes are, or will shortly be, Russia, Italy, and probably Japan and New Zealand. These arrangements are criticized *infra* 4.4.
3. This conclusion leaves us, it will be seen, with only two puzzles: i) whether the German system is truly 'mixed' and, ii) the proper classification of the Japanese electoral system. See *infra* 2.2 and 2.4.

4. Preferential or preference voting allows voters to indicate on their ballots one or more preferred (selected) candidates either by writing in or ticking off their names. Generally preference voting applies to PR list systems. When applied to the alternative vote it also entails a rank-ordering of the preferred candidates that is not contemplated, instead, by the PR list systems.

5. These proportionality rankings are disputed. I basically follow the assessment of Lijphart (1986). I neglect here the Imperiali and many other conceivable PR methods, which are accounted for in most electoral textbooks.

6. This is a rule of thumb. As Douglas Rae correctly points out (1971, pp. 117–18), the relation between greater size and greater proportionality is curvilinear, not linear. However the size factor remains the major variable for the stretch that includes most real world constituency sizes.

7. Thus in the Netherlands representation is denied in practice only to a party that does not obtain the support of 1/150 of the voters (which equals 0.67 percent).

8. Countries with the lowest constituency sizes are: Chile (2-member), Ireland and Japan (3- to 5-member). The Japanese perceive their districts as medium-sized, and this is because their yardstick is their previous system. However, from a comparative standpoint the Japanese districts have been – within PR – almost as small as they can conceivably be.

9. The additional member system can be conceived and construed as a PR system in its own right. Thus far, however, it has only been implemented (in Germany) as a 'correction' to the distortions arising from plurality voting in single-member districts. I thus confine my illustration of PR to list systems and to STV.

10. Alternatively, voters may be permitted to vary the order of candidates on the party list. This provision is called *panachage*. In any event, with any kind of preference voting every vote goes to the party list.

11. I neglect the sub-clauses, so to speak, of the *Sperrklausel*, which vary from country to country.

12. Almost no Greek election (before and after the seven year colonel's dictatorship, 1967–1974) has been carried out under exactly the same electoral law; and the swings go all the way from PR to plurality in 1952, then to a plurality-PR mix in 1956, and subsequently back to various PR arrangements. On

the point – thresholds – their peak has been in 1958: 25 percent for single parties, 35 percent for two-party alliances, and 40 percent for larger alliances. Peaks aside, Greece has long been travelling at a 15–17 level of exclusion for single parties, and respectively 25 and 30–40 percent exclusions for the other two cases (see Seferiades, 1986). In the October 1993 election, however, the exclusion for a single party was down at the 3 percent level.

13. I am assuming here that the second round is not closed to the top two finishers, but open to 3–4 contenders. I explain this *infra* 4.3.

14. In 1986 a sleight of hand of Mitterrand imposed a brief return to PR (with small constituencies and a 5 percent threshold) intended to favor the electoral chances of his party. But the double ballot was immediately reinstated.

15. Unfortunately, a number of scholars associate bipolar with polarization, and thus use 'bipolar' and 'bipolarized' interchangeably. But no. A bipolar system is assumed not to be polarized, while a bipolar polarization denotes a highly conflictual and breakdown-prone polity. Technically put, a bipolar system assumes a normal, bell-curve distribution (a Gauss–Laplace curve) of where the electors place themselves along a left-right (or other) continuum, whereas bipolarization assumes a double-peaked distribution of political opinion with an almost empty center.

2 Who Gets Elected?

2.1 PERSON VOTING AND LIST VOTING

Thus far electoral systems have been classified, in the main, on the basis of how votes are translated into seats. But what about who gets elected? How does one become a candidate and then win office?

Concerning these questions the rule of thumb is that candidates come forward on their own resources (financial and/or other) only when a party system is feeble, feebly structured, and highly decentralized. The United States and Brazil are two eminent cases in point. To be sure, the self-proposing candidate is such with respect to party control. Since he or she can seldom make it on wealth alone (their personal wealth), in most instances the self-propelled runner is linked with and supported by unions, religious groups, interest groups or indeed 'idea groups'. However, dependence on other-than-party organizations still counts as independence from party.

In any event, more often than not candidates get on the ballot on the basis of their within-party force and as a result of party infightings.[1] And when this is the case, it is appropriate to speak of party conditioned and party dependent candidatures. In short, here the nominating agent is the party.

One often hears that the democratic manner of breaking through the alternative between self-appointment (as qualified above) and party appointment is the _primary system_, that is, the candidate selection process characteristically adopted in the United States. The democratic value of a grass roots, pre-electoral selection of the electoral candidates cannot be doubted, even though one may argue that the 'intense publics' that participate in this selection are an exceedingly small and distorted sample of the universe that will ultimately vote. One may further argue that by now primaries are overly conditioned and manipulated by media interference.[2] However that may be, the sure thing is that primaries were deliberately introduced to weaken the party 'oligarchy' (the smoke-filled rooms that searched for the winning horse). By the same token, primaries work best when parties perform least. And in this connection whoever believes that the American primary can be successfully exported to other countries must confront the fact American parties are quite unique in being parties without card-carrying members. In the United States a person is a democrat or a republican on one's own recognition, simply by declaring (verbally) that his or her party loyalty goes to such and such. Per contra, most parties in most of the world, and especially the well structured mass parties, are made of duly registered members whose application is screened by the party.

This being so, one can hardly imagine, around the world, open primaries with cross-party crossover. I shall tell shortly the horror story of how the Italian preferential voting has been abused and utterly twisted; and I can easily imagine similar horror scenarios of how open primaries might perform in export. In most of the world prudence would recommend, then, closed primaries. If so, however, there is no assurance that intra-party life will be significantly affected. The rule of thumb seems to be that the stronger the party organization and the more the campaign funds are in some manner party controlled, the more the primary process will be party manipulated, loses its democratic value, and again creates party dependent candidates.

So much on how one enters the running. But let us narrow the question to, How does a candidate get elected? The relevant distinction is, on this score, between person voting and list voting; and the related assumptions are that when we vote for persons, who is who (with what credentials) makes a difference and may become a decisive factor, whereas where we vote for lists we basically vote a party (its symbol, ideology, program, platform) and the party largely controls, in turn, the individual winning. By and large both assumptions are correct, but only if they are duly qualified.

Person voting characterizes majoritarian single-member district systems (thereby including the double ballot ones). To be sure, even here candidates are, as a rule, party members chosen via party channels. Yet in districts that elect only one member, voters do concretely see concrete persons with proper names. But this 'seeing' does not in itself establish that person matters more than party. With single-member constituencies parties must bow to the need of searching for a 'good candidate' wherever it can be found if, and only if, the constituency is unsafe, that is to say, if the plurality edge is small and up for grabs. With safe constituencies in which a given party enjoys, election after election, a comfortable majority, parties are no longer hard pressed to seek whoever is best (for winning); they can afford to propose their insiders. The question thus turns on what makes a constituency 'safe'. Here the argument currently is that in most traditional Western democracies party identifications and identifiers are on the wane; and this entails that safe constituencies are equally on the wane. However, in the United States the melting pot no longer 'melts' and therefore ethnic 'block voting' is on the rise; ethnicity and language are back in other countries as well as powerful coagulants; and ideological or other identifications are still strong in the new or less stable democracies. As the old safe constituencies become unsafe, new ones are in the making.

Be that as it may, the general point remains that single-member districts require parties to pay at least some heed to the personality traits of the candidate. The Roman emperor Caligula appointed senator his horse; and in electoral politics the expression 'horse of Caligula' conveys that any 'nobody' (even a horse) can get himself elected. But horses of Caligula are less easily elected with single person voting than with list systems in multi-member constituencies.

Turning to the PR list systems, the relevant distinction becomes whether the party slates are closed or open (to preferential voting). Clearly, party control over the selection and election of its candidates is maximal when the lists are closed, that is, when the rank-ordering of the names on the slate is preordained and cannot be altered by the voter. Instead open lists with preference voting are assumed to put the electorate in control of the selection process.[3] But we cannot be too sure of that. Just like strong parties with machine-based mobilizational capacity circumvent primaries, by the same token they easily circumvent the intent of preference voting by seeing to it that preferences are duly concentrated on their machine bosses.

With this caveat in mind, it is worth looking into the Italian experience with preference voting between 1948 and 1992 in some detail, for here we have a case that has gone far beyond any normal deviation. Since most Italian constituencies allowed each voter to indicate three preferences, assigning each voter a different combination of three numbers became a way of identifying and controlling his or her vote. This stratagem was invented early on by the Communist party, and subsequently became, in the South, a control device employed by the Mafia and mafia-like networks. A further, unintended outcome of the Italian preference voting is that it quickly opened the doors to massive ballot stuffing. When the votes were counted, the party members sitting at each electoral seat did make sure that the attribution of the party vote was faultless, but closed their eyes on each other on the marking on the ballot of additional preferences. In this way each party assured the election of the candidates of its own choice by cheating with the voter's indication. Note that these abuses were known to all the interested parties; and yet no cure was either sought or found for them until preference voting was entirely eliminated in 1993.

2.2   THE GERMAN AND THE HARE SYSTEMS

Is there no way – other than preference voting – to combine PR with a personalization of the vote? The standard answer is that both the German electoral system and the single transferable vote (STV) perform as 'personalized PR systems'.

The German system (as of 1953) is a very peculiar and often misunderstood arrangement. For the *Bundestag*, voters are given two ballots: with one they elect half of the Chamber as the English do (in plurality single-member constituencies); with the other ballot they elect the remaining half of the *Bundestag* on the basis of national PR closed party lists.

However, the overall distribution of seats turns out to be (for the parties that pass the 5 percent barrier) entirely proportional. This is so because the allocation of the federal parliamentary seats is calculated exclusively on the basis of the list votes (the votes obtained by the parties on the second ballot).[4]

Most observers display the German formula as being a 'mixed' majority–PR system. Yes; but, more importantly, No. No because the mixture of its ingredients does not entail a mixed product. As I was saying, the outcome is perfectly proportional. Note that the German electoral system is misunderstood, on this score, not only by its foreign admirers but by the German voters themselves; for surveys show that most voters miss that the second vote is the crucial one (for the allocation of seats) and believe it instead to be an indication of their second preference.[5] Let it be reiterated, therefore, that the German system must be understood, in substance, as a PR system that obtains (for half of its *Bundestag* members) a person-based selection.[6]

Many observers misunderstand the German arrangement on another score as well, by wrongly crediting it with a reductive effect on the number of parties, whereas the fact that Germany has long enjoyed a three-party format has nothing to do with the aforesaid majoritarian component of its electoral system. The reduction to just three of the parties of the Bonn Republic has instead a great deal to do with the fact that the Constitutional Court outlawed as anti-democratic, and therefore as unconstitutional, both the Communist and the Neo-Nazi parties. With these two major contenders out of the way, it became easy for the *Sperrklause* to dispose of the smaller brush. So, the true merit of the German system is not that it reduces party fragmentation, but that it succeeds in 'personalizing' the electoral choice of the voter better (or more securely) than preference voting with PR list systems.

However, the complete personalization of PR voting is afforded by the *single transferable vote* (STV), also known as the *Hare system*; for here party lists are eliminated entirely. As we already know (*supra* 1.4), under STV voters write the names of their candidates in order of preference with no reference to party names or symbols. Any vote surplus is reallocated according to the second preferences; and the bottom candidates are successively eliminated and their preferences redistributed until all the seats are filled. Needless to say, the Hare system is perfectly proportional. However, while STV was conceived in order to weaken party influence, this intent has been defeated by party strength. The Hare system has been employed in Ireland since 1922, and is equally used for Australia's Senate and in Malta. In all these instances party lines are very seldom crossed and party identifications prevail, that is, voters well know which candidates stand for which parties and vote accordingly (see Bogdanor and Butler, 1983, pp. 8–12).

Is that it? No, because Japan too has (had until 1993) an electoral system strictly based on person voting. But into which kind or type of electoral system does Japan fall? The answers vary and are, for the most part, fuzzy and inaccurate. The actual proceedings are these: that the Japanese voter is handed a blank ballot on which he or she is required to write only the name of a candidate, and one name only. Note that no indication is given, on the ballot paper, of who the candidates are, let alone their party affiliation. There is no question, then, that here we have person voting. Thereafter in each district three to five candidates are elected on the basis of their having received the highest shares of the turnout. So, what kind of electoral system is this? At the moment let me simply point out that while the single transferable vote and the Japanese formula both attest to how we can have PR without recourse to party lists, nonetheless in both cases the voters do know the party affiliations of the candidates and do implicitly vote party. The point is thus confirmed that party strength remains a decisive variable under whatever electoral arrangement.

2.3   MINORITY REPRESENTATION AND GERRYMANDERING

Aside from who gets elected how (individual representation) a related concern is to favor the representation of minority parties and/or of minorities (bloc representation). In theory the best methods for this purpose would seem to be cumulative and/or point voting in multi-member constituencies. With cumulative voting each voter is given as many votes as there are seats to fill, and is allowed to distribute them as he or she pleases and eventually to give them all to one candidate. With *point voting* the voter is given more votes (points) than there are seats to be filled, and is then allowed to rank order the candidates by allocating the points among them. The two techniques are similar – with point voting being the more sophisticated one – and both allow minority voters to win representation by concentrating their votes or points.[7] But these largely remain proposals awaiting enactment. In the real world the two most frequent techniques aimed at securing minority representation, or at least at reducing 'majority victory', are i) the limited vote, and ii) *ad hoc* districting.

The *limited vote* consists, remember, of giving electors – in multi-member constituencies – more than one but still fewer votes than there are seats to fill. The limited vote is partially employed in Spain (for 197 out of 239 Senators); and in many texts one reads that the Japanese electoral system for the Lower House is also a variant of the limited vote (e.g., Bogdanor and Butler, 1983, p. ix). But how can that be? As we have seen, the Japanese voter is allowed one vote, and one vote only, in constituencies that elect on average four members; and the winners simply are the three, four or five candidates which have obtained in their constituencies the highest number of votes (on the one man, one vote basis). Therefore to consider the Japanese formula a variant of the limited vote is to violate a defining characteristic of the latter.

Aside from the limited vote, proper, the other way of enhancing minority representation is, I have said, *ad hoc* districting, that is, a drawing of constituency boundaries that intentionally fabricates winning pluralities. The American traditional name, or nickname, for this practice is Gerrymandering (from a Massachusetts Governor Gerry, who in 1812 first had the astute idea of drawing a salamander-shaped district that brought together his voters and dispersed his opponents). Now, it should be clear that Gerrymandering is an abuse, a shameful rigging. But this rigging has acquired in the United States a court-enforced legitimacy and also a rationale, a reason for being, as a means of securing ethnic representation (especially for black, but also for hispanic concentrations). Thus one currently finds, in the United States, electoral districts that look like Rorschach blots.[8]

I personally believe that good intentions should not be served by bad means, and that manipulations of constituency boundaries that intentionally fabricate preordained winners come very close to being frauds. I thus find Gerrymandering an indefensible practice even when serving a 'civil rights' cause; especially because point voting, cumulative voting, or a correctly understood and well conceived limited vote would serve the same purpose without abuse. To be sure, these alternative routes to minority protection and representation require multi-member districts, while Gerrymandering performs at its best with single-member districts. But no great harm would follow from the adoption – in the particular areas where ethnic minorities remain underrepresented – of (say) three-member constituencies in which voters are given two cumulable votes.

2.4   A CODA ON JAPAN

Now back to Japan and to the question as to how the electoral system it practiced until 1993 has to be understood and classified. Let me quote on the matter – with reference to Japan and Spain – Lijphart and others (in Grofman and Lijphart eds., 1986, pp. 154–55), who write:

> The limited vote uses multimember districts in which each voter has fewer votes than there are seats; when each voter has only one vote [!], the limited vote may be called the single non-transferable vote. The winners are those candidates who have collected the largest number of votes. Hence the limited vote appears very similar to plurality [!]. It also has some of the principal advantages claimed for plurality, especially the fact that the voters vote for individual

candidates . . . The limited vote is in fact frequently called a plurality method . . . We prefer a stricter definition of plurality system which specifies that the voters have as many votes as the number of seats available in the district [!] . . . The most important difference is that the limited vote does, whereas plurality does not facilitate minority representation. In this respect, the limited vote resembles PR. It is therefore more accurate to call the limited vote, including SNTV (the single non-transferable vote) a semiproportional system rather than a plurality system.

Quite frankly, and as my exclamation marks underscore, I am unable to make heads or tails of the above. Certainly I deny – I have already done so – that the single non-transferable vote (SNTV) can and should be considered a variety of the limited vote. I also find much of the overall argument confused and mistaken. I agree, however, that the Japanese system can be classified as an SNTV system, for it is in fact the case that the Japanese voter does have a single personalized vote that cannot be transferred. But why oscillate between a plurality and a PR interpretation of SNTV?

In my understanding the Japanese electoral system definitely is (was) a PR system characterized by personalized voting (and thus an SNTV system) and by small constituencies (and thus by disproportional PR). The system is proportional – under my definition (*supra* 1.1) – in that it elects ordinally the candidates that receive the highest portions (proportions) of the turnout of their districts. It does, however, limit the number of parties because the magnitude of its multi-member districts is small. We may want to call this a 'semi-proportional' outcome. But this label simply underscores the general rule that the proportionality of PR decreases as the district size decreases.

The complications that have complicated the understanding of Japan's case do not reside in its electoral system, but – I submit – in the Japanese party system and in the manner in which its predominant protagonist (the LDP) has carved its way into an SNTV arrangement. To wit, in order to attain and maintain its absolute majority of parliamentary seats the

LDP has to win for itself an average of two seats out of four. In principle, SNTV is supposed to hurt large parties and to favor medium-sized ones. In part this intent is accomplished. Assuming a four-member constituency (the average size), the vote cost of the last winner, the fourth one, ranges at the 20 percent level (and can descend to 15 percent in the five-member constituencies). But the aforesaid intent is also largely defied by the LDP's ability to steer clear of two miscalculations, respectively, overnomination (presenting too many candidates that are all defeated) and undernomination (wasting too many votes on a single candidate).[9] And this exploitation of the electoral system brings about very negative side-effects. For the arrangement prompts a candidate-centered competition, that is, bitter infighting among candidates of the same party, and thus a very high degree of intra-party divisiveness. This is tantamount to saying that the LDP obtains a highly fractionalized and factionalized structure: it is less a party *with* factions and more a party *of* factions.[10] Indeed, the very financing of politics – which has become enormously expensive – is almost entirely channeled within the factions and directly to the incumbents.[11]

While the Japanese electoral system does not require, I believe, the tortuous explanations displayed by the literature, still it has evolved in a manner that serves no purpose and that engenders more drawbacks than advantages. The Japanese are well advised to drop it. Whether their new electoral system is a well advised one is, however, a different matter (see *infra* 4.4).

NOTES

1. With decentralized parties these infightings occur at the local level; with centralized parties they can be largely decided at the national level. Thus decentralized parties disperse but are also likely to multiply intra-party conflicts.

2. The literature on the primaries is astonishingly poor. In *Southern Politics* (1949) and in *American State Politics* (1956) V. O. Key

was highly critical of their workings. In the Sixties primaries became a progressive taboo, and scholars have seemingly been wary of investigating the topic. The *International Social Science Encyclopedia* of 1968 does not even have the entry!

3. Note that open list systems allow for different degrees of 'opening'. Aside from *panachage*, much depends (as we shall see in assessing the Italian experience) on how many preferences the voters are allowed. Technically, the party slates can be rank-ordered, or may suggest only one preferred candidate at the top of the list (the so-called *case de tête*), or may instead enumerate all the names of the candidates in a pure and simple alphabetical order.

4. The discrepancies thus resulting are resolved by the already cited additional member system, that is, by providing additional seats in parliament for the parties that gain more constituency seats in any one *Land* (regional state) than the total to which their share of the vote would entitle them. The PR calculations are based on the D'Hondt algorithm. I omit the details and the intricacies of this system, which are neatly summarized, e.g., by Max Kaase (in Lijphart and Grofman, 1984b, pp. 157–58).

5. This misperception has in fact helped the Free Democrats, i.e. the liberals, to survive, pushing them above the 5 percent exclusion.

6. However, the fact that the German formula creates two kinds of MP – those elected by constituencies, and those elected from party lists – is of no consequence to their parliamentary role, for the members of the first group are not expected to be constituency-serving members and are not involved in constituency work any more than the list-elected representatives. For a critical evaluation of PR-majority 'mixes' see *infra* 4.4.

7. I neglect special arrangements, such as the establishment of electoral districts reserved for minority voters, as in New Zealand for Maori voters (see Lijphart, 1984b, pp. 211–13).

8. Note that 'the use of computers brought a new degree of sophistication to boundary manipulation. . . . In state after state, grotesquely shaped districts . . . are justified by politicians and approved by judges with the solemn chant, "one person, one vote"' (G.E. Baker, in Grofman, Lijphart eds., 1986, p. 271).

9. Remember that all of this holds up to the July 1993 election at which the LDP split and lost its absolute majority at the *Diet*

(the lower Chamber). In all likelihood the new electoral system will close 38 years of unbroken Liberal-Democratic rule.

10. In Sartori (1976, pp. 76–88) I criticize the indiscriminate use of 'faction' to describe within-party divisions, and suggest 'fraction' as a general neutral term. But here this discussion is immaterial.

11. I explain this in some detail in Sartori (1976) pp. 88–93.

3 The Importance of Electoral Systems

3.1 HOW IMPORTANT?

The importance of electoral systems has long been down-graded. A large majority of scholars have argued i) that they are not an independent variable, and/or ii) that their effects are, at best, uncertain. Both arguments are demonstrably wrong.

In 1958 Grumm concluded his review of Duverger's laws on the effects of electoral systems (*infra* 3.2), suggesting that 'PR is a result rather than a cause of the party system' (p. 375). In 1963 Eckstein's insight was that perhaps 'electoral systems only express the deeper determinants of society' (p. 253). Twenty years later Vernon Bogdanor still affirmed that 'any theory making the electoral system a fundamental causative factor in the development of party systems cannot be sustained', and concluded that 'electoral systems must be understood against the background of a society's historical development, which is in turn profoundly affected by political choices' (1983, pp. 254, 261).

Now, in a causal argument nothing is uncaused: everything is caused by something but, in turn, the consequence of something becomes the cause of something else. Thus to argue that electoral systems are 'caused' does not imply that at that moment the causal chain is broken. The presumption is, rather, that once in place electoral systems become causative factors that produce, at their turn, consequences of conse-quence. Indeed, if electoral systems were of little consequence why on earth would politicians fight so bitterly about them? And why would reformers fight so persistently to have them changed? Much ado about nothing?

Another argument has been that even if we recognize that electoral systems matter, the fact remains that electoral systems cannot 'be constructed deliberately and changed freely', and that the discussions about them 'feign a freedom of choice that really does not exist' (Nohlen, 1984b, p. 217; see also Katz, 1980, p. 123). In building this case Nohlen and others confine their scrutiny to Europe in the post World War Two period, minimize important changes that have occurred within the context of PR, and win their case on the evidence that during the aforesaid period majoritarian systems have remained majoritarian and that only France has reverted from PR to a double ballot plurality system. But this is indeed incomplete and thin evidence. What about previous periods? And what about other areas? In any event, the events of the 1990s amply suffice to rend the 'no choice' argument in tatters. With the fall of communism, the dismemberment of the Soviet Union and Yugoslavia, the growing, if reluctant, acceptance of pro forma democratic elections in African countries, and with new states (tiny as they may be) sprinkling all around, we are currently confronted with far more beginnings from scratch that involve *per force* choice, than the 17 cases on which Nohlen builds his case. And the deadly blow to the unchangeability argument comes with the 1993 Italian turnaround (an unprecedented leap from PR back to a plurality single ballot system).[1]

To be sure, change by reform is always difficult. Once an electoral arrangement is in place, its beneficiaries protect their vested interests and try hard to go on playing the game by the rules that they know. The fact nonetheless remains that electoral systems are in fact being installed and/or variously modified in many areas of today's world. Thus the pressing question of a time of change becomes: Do changers know how to change whatever they seek to change? And, narrowing the question to the issue at hand, Whence and how do present-day electoral system-makers (or remakers) seek inspiration? By looking at the cleavage structure of their societies? By excavating into the deeper determinants of their history? Of course not. Across the world electoral system-makers look scantily around at external models, scantily ask for expert advice from self-styled experts, and end up adopting the system that in their own understanding is perceived as being in their own immediate advantage – with many hurrays to history, social determinants and noble traditions.

There is little that scholars can do with regard to the politicians' self-interests – other than showing that they are or might be wrongly understood. Still, scholars are supposed and required to give sound advice – regardless of whether it is being heeded. And here is the rub: are present-day political scientists capable of giving sound advice? On the views that I have briefly reviewed, the answer must be no. A profession that has long held that electoral systems cannot start anything (since they are caused by politics but cannot cause politics), or cannot be changed (the 'no choice' argument), and (most damningly of all) whose canon has unwaveringly been that their effects cannot be predicted with any precision or confidence – a profession that has long held such views cannot have in store much advice to give. The truth is, I submit, that our alleged electoral experts have largely failed to develop the expertise that is required of them, and that much of their current counseling is poor or plainly wrong. As I propose to show – beginning with showing (contrary to the prevailing wisdom) that the effects of electoral systems can be adequately predicted and determined.

3.2 THE EFFECTS OF ELECTORAL SYSTEMS: A DISCUSSION

What is it that electoral systems actually do, that is, what are their effects on what? Whatever causes them, what is it that they cause? Duverger, who was the first author to address these questions, formulated the following two laws: first, 'The majority [plurality] single ballot system tends to party dualism'; and, second, 'The double ballot majority system and proportional representation tend to multipartism' (1954, pp. 247 and 269).[2] In truth, Duverger did not call his two generalizations 'laws' (but formulas or schemes). However, they have become known as Duverger's laws and – wording aside – that is what they are meant to be. It should also be clarified from the outset that Duverger's second law definitely implies that PR has 'multiplying effects' (see Duverger 1954, pp. 279, 281, 282). In essence, then, Duverger proposes two laws. The first one states that plurality (majoritarian) systems tend to party dualism. The second law asserts that PR tends to multipartism, i.e., that it has a multiplying effect.[3]

It has been easy to tear Duverger's formulas and their demonstration to pieces. For one, Duverger assumes that a causal relation can be warranted by a correlation; that is to say, he misses the difference between 'cause of' and 'associated with'. In the second place a causal generalization is verifiable if, and only if, the cause and the effect are clearly specified, whereas the effect of Duverger's first law (party dualism) defies underpinning, and the effect of his second law (multipartism) also suffers from excessive imprecision. The point thus is that laws that posit effects on the number of parties must establish *how their number is determined.* Instead, Duverger never abides by any consistent counting rule. At times he counts all the parties at their face value; at other times he dismisses some parties as local, half-parties, or presumably ephemeral. In sum: since the effect of the assumed causal factor is never pinned down, Duverger can all too easily tailor his evidence as being a confirming one. Even so, his laws remain crippled by exceptions.

That Duverger's laws can be easily torn to pieces (as happens with most first tries) is hardly a reason for giving up trying. Yet a crushing majority of scholars have been content with showing that Duverger was mistaken.[4] Interest in electoral systems was revived in the 1980s, especially under the relentless impulse of Lijphart.[5] But in spite of this revived interest, to this day the discipline goes along, by and large, with the conclusion that 'the relationships between electoral systems, party systems, and the process of social change . . . are not such as can be summed up in scientific laws . . . The comparative study of electoral systems and party systems is likely to be of more use in shedding light on what is unique . . . than in yielding generalizations. . .' (Bogdanor and Butler, 1983, p. 261). The prevailing wisdom of the profession still is, then, that comparatively valid generalizations are impossible to achieve.

Really? Let us give the matter another try.[6] And let us begin from the beginning, that is, with defining the concept of law.

In the social science realm 'laws' are generalizations endowed with explanatory power that detect a regularity. The 'explanatory power' clause is crucial in that it underpins the difference between scientific and statistical laws. The latter do quantify well confirmed frequencies, but do not obtain explanatory power. To know that the average life span of humans is, say, seventy years does not explain anything. And the rule of thumb regarding explanatory power is that the force of an explanation is greater the more a law definitely asserts cause–effect relationships. The bottom line is, then, that a law is required to declare more than a regularity and cannot consist of a mere generalization. Furthermore, since a law stands so long as it is not falsified, it must be formulated in ways that permit empirical confirmation and disconfirmation. Finally, a crucial difference among laws is whether they predict single events or only classes of events; and it goes without saying that the former laws have greater value than the latter ones.

Now, most social science laws do not predict single events. However, the laws on the influence of electoral systems (cause) upon the number of parties (effect) are supposed to do just that, i.e., to apply to *all* and *each* electoral event. But if that is the case, then our laws are improperly tested by frequencies and correlation coefficients. Statistical testing is appropriate for laws that apply to classes of events, but has only subsidiary value when a law is assumed to predict discrete outcomes. And this entails that the test is, here, the *exception*, that is to say, cases that do not fall under the rule, that make exception to the rule. To illustrate, Douglas Rae submits Duverger's first law (on the effects of majoritarian systems) to a correlational testing that finds that 'of . . . 107 cases, 89.7% fall into the predicted categories of association'; and Rae comments that this 'suggests a relationship which is somewhat weaker than the term 'sociological law' might lead one to expect, but is, nevertheless, a strong association' (1971, p. 94). The association is indeed strong; but it cannot establish whether we have a law and whether it is weak or not. Thus it is Rae's instinct (rather than his methodology) that immediately and correctly leads him to probe the matter on the basis of the 'exceptional cases'. The question remains how exceptions are to be handled.

To be sure, if a law is assumed to be *deterministic* – meaning that given the cause the effect is also given, and thus is known and certain *ex ante* – then even a single exception suffices to kill the law. But social science laws cannot be and never are deterministic,[7] and can therefore withstand some deviation. However, even if a non-deterministic law is not *eo ipso* killed by its exceptions (if they are truly such), even so exceptions are always troubling and do pose a puzzle. The puzzle can be disposed of in either one of two ways: by entering a necessary condition that restricts the applicability of the law (and, if so, the exception no longer subsists), or by incorporating the exception(s) into a reformulation of the law that subsumes them. Since this is how I propose in fact to proceed, the two strategies will be explained in due course. Assume, however, that neither strategy works, that exceptions remain. It is only at this residual point, I submit, that *ad hoc* considerations offer grounds for claiming that a law is enfeebled but not quite falsified by such and such exceptions.

3.3   THE INFLUENCE OF ELECTORAL SYSTEMS RESTATED

Electoral systems have a two-fold effect: one on the voter, and one on the number of parties. These effects must be assessed separately, for the number of parties does not derive only from the behavior of the voters, but also from how their votes are transformed into parliamentary seats.[8] The effect on the voters is generally described as a restraining, manipulative, constraining, or even coercive impact (in a feeble sense of the term). Let us settle for *constraining effect* and note that this effect ranges from strongly constraining (with majoritarian systems) to utterly unconstraining (with pure PR). In the latter case the electoral system simply has no effect – and that closes the matter.

Turning to the effect of the electoral system on the number of parties, this impact is best called *reductive effect*, for either their number is reduced, or the electoral system turns out to be ineffectual. (There is, we shall see, no multiplying effect.) And this reduction too ranges from being strong to feeble. Here we must pause, however, to settle a preliminary point, namely, *how parties are to be counted*. For it is positively misleading to count all the parties that materialize in any given party system at face value.

A would-be authoritative source dispenses its wisdom on electoral reform on the basis of the following counting (of parties). 'For party-list countries: Italy, 15; Israel, 12; Sweden, 7; Germany, 6; for various systems: Ireland (STV), 6; Japan, 6; France, 4; Australia (ATV), 3; for simple plurality countries: India, 16; Britain, 8; Canada, 4; United States, 2.'[9] However, these numbers are worse than meaningless, for they undercut the very possibility of identifying party systems in their distinctive nature and, to be sure, of searching for what brings them about. If Britain has eight parties, how can it be that there are still fools around that believe in the notion of a two-party system? If PR Italy has 15 parties, and first-past-the-post India has 16, why bother about electoral systems? Well, for whoever bothers about them it is, or should be, obvious that evidence such as the above makes no sense and inexorably develops into nonsense. The fact is that in every polity one finds irrelevant parties that make no difference, that can appear or disappear without even being noticed. Britain does not have eight parties that carry weight, nor Italy 15, nor Ireland or Germany six. So, how do we sort out, by which criteria, the *relevant parties*, the parties that determine the nature of the party system? To this end I have proposed the two counting rules that follow.

'*Rule 1.* A minor party can be discounted as irrelevant whenever it remains over time superfluous, in the sense that it is never needed or put to use for any feasible coalition majority. Conversely, a minor party must be counted, no matter how small it is, if it finds itself in a position to determine over time, or at some point in time, at least one of the possible governmental majorities.' However, this rule applies only to the parties that are governing oriented and/or ideologically acceptable to the other coalition partners. Therefore a second, subsidiary and broader rule is needed for the opposition-oriented or ideologically incompatible parties. *Rule 2*. A party qualifies for relevance whenever its existence or appearance affects the tactics of party competition, and particularly when it alters the direction of competition . . . either leftward, rightward or in both directions, of the governing oriented parties' (Sartori, 1976, pp. 122–3). In short, then, relevant parties must either have a *coalition potential* (as per Rule 1), or a *blackmail potential* (as per Rule 2). Parties that have neither are irrelevant, and ought not be counted.[10]

It should go without saying – but it is perhaps better to say it – that the above counting rules apply to, and are devised for, parliamentary systems. The reason for this is that it is in parliamentary systems – not in presidential systems – that governments reflect parliamentary majorities and that the 'governing function' becomes strongly conditioned by how many parties enter a government. This is not to say that the number of relevant parties becomes unimportant with presidential systems. I shall argue, for instance, that presidentialism is likely to perform better with few than with many parties (*infra* 11.2). But here the counting criteria must be reformulated and relaxed, for the parties that count are simply the ones that make a difference in helping (or obstructing) the president's election, and that determine his having (or not having) a majority support in the legislative assemblies.

There are two major quantitative-mathematical alternatives to the counting rules that I propose. One is the 'index of fractionalization', or F index, devised by Douglas Rae (1971, pp. 53–58 and *passim*); the other is the 'effective number of parties' measure devised by Taagepera and Shugart (1989, pp. 77–91). Rae's index indicates the probability that any two members of a parliament (if this is the referent) will belong to different parties; varies from zero (total concentration; there is only one party) to a maximum of one (as many parties as there are seats); and basically measures the number of parties through their size.[11] The technical flaw is that the measure actually overvalues the larger parties and compresses too quickly the smaller ones. And the substantive defects are that the measure is insensitive both to the 'position values' of parties and to the 'cleavage differences' among them.[12]

Taagepera's and Shugart's measure of the 'effective number of parties' is more straightforward than Rae's. We need, they argue, 'an operational definition of the number of electoral parties that depends on nothing other than the vote shares'; measure the 'relative sizes' of parties by letting the vote shares 'determine their own weights' (e.g., a party with 40 percent of the votes also receives a weight of .40, so that its weighted value is $.40 \times .40 = .16$); and end up with an index (the Herfindahl–Hirschman, HH for short, concentration index) resulting from the adding up of the weighted values for all party votes (1989, pp. 78–9). While the Taagepera–Shugart route is different from Rae's, the information (and, by the same token, the loss of information) is just about the same in both approaches. Indeed, as the authors themselves recognize, 'the concentration index HH also leads to . . . the Rae fractionalization index' (*loc. cit.*, p. 80).

Are the fractionalization and/or concentration measures substitutes for my counting rules? Rae's index has certainly carried to the last man the computer-addicted profession. While we relax, the F index produces numerical values that dispense with, and dispose of, the need of substantive knowledge. Better still, numerical precision is assumed to be unfailingly superior to so-called qualitative knowledge. Understandably, it is hard to resist such sirens. I resist, however. I agree that continuous measures of party size convey useful information that my counting rules do not provide.[13] However, my criteria are sensitive to other aspects: first of all, the *position value* of parties. To illustrate, parties such as the German liberals (in the 6 percent range), the Italian Republicans (in the 3 percent range) or the Israeli small and fractured religious parties, almost disappear in the Rae measure, while they have definitely been – on account of their pivotal positioning – systemically relevant parties. Secondly, my criteria also detect the cleavage difference between *in-parties* and *out-parties*, that is to say, between coalition-available (relatively close) and coalition-excluded (distant and/or anti-system) parties; a difference that indicates, in turn, whether we are confronted with a non-polarized or instead a polarized fragmentation; and a difference to which both the F and HH indexes are monumentally insensitive. Let it be added that in matters (such as voting and parties) where easy intelligibility is of crucial importance, the wholesale loss of concreteness that comes with mathematical formulas is a very severe handicap. Admittedly, my concreteness is somewhat loose and impressionistic; but it cannot be as misleading as a mathematical precision that is only too often a false precision fabricated by the measurement (see, e.g., Vanhanen, 1990).

Be that as it may, my criteria assess the *systemic relevance* of parties; the indexes of Rae (and others) do not. So, how can it be held that the latter are replacements of the former? Awaiting this contention to be sustained, it should be understood that in the 'laws' that I am about to put forward reference to two-, three-, four-, five- and more-than-five party systems applies to 'relevant parties' sorted out by my counting rules.

Resuming the thread of the argument, let us begin with the major instance of majoritarian electoral systems: the plurality single-member district system. Here the voter's choice is constrained and restricted (unless he prefers to waste his vote) to the front-runners. It is truly the case, then, that the 'first-past-the-post system' does manufacture, constituency by constituency, two-party (or two-candidate) competition. But if the voter is pressed, *where he votes*, into a two-cornered choice, this does not entail in the least that a corresponding reduction of the number of national parties necessarily follows. The restraining effect on the voter is not the same as an overall reduction effect on the total number of parties. The reason – it bears repetition – very simply is that the voter is constrained on a constituency basis. Therefore neither a plurality nor any majoritarian system can reduce the relevant number of national parties to two, unless the same two parties happen to be the relevant contestants in all the constituencies. The problem thus is: how does local two-partism become state-wide two-partism? Clearly, the argument that plurality elections 'tend to' a two-party system has missed, so far, a *necessary condition*. And this missing condition, factor or variable is the party system itself. The egg of Columbus can now stand up without falling.

It is not only the electoral system but also the party system that conditions the voter. And the argument that applies to the former equally applies to the latter. We have noted that electoral systems are variously constraining (*vis-à-vis* voters) and variously reductive (*vis-à-vis* parties). On both counts electoral systems can be divided into 'strong' (strongly effective) and 'feeble' (feebly effective).[14] In similar fashion also party systems can be dichotomized into strong and feeble, depending on whether they are, as systems, structured or unstructured. The point thus is that the effects of electoral systems cannot be correctly assessed without assessing at the same time the manipulative and channeling properties of the party system as such.

The issue turns on what we mean by 'structured system' and, thereby, on the conditions that are conducive to a strong, i.e. strongly structured, party system. So long as the voter purely and simply votes for the local notable or for some kind of local chieftain (in the *personalismo* context spoken of in Latin America), parties remain labels of little, if any, consequence. Hence, as long as these conditions prevail, the party system is not structured. However, when allegiance is given to the party more than to notables or chieftains, that is, when the voter relates to abstract party images, at this moment it is no longer the individual boss or leader that 'elects' the party, but the party that elects (puts into office) the individual. As the process develops, it is the party system that becomes perceived as a natural *system of channelment* of the political society. And when the electorate takes for granted a given set of political routes and alternatives very much as drivers take for granted a given system of highways, then a party system has reached the stage of structural consolidation qua system.

How a structured party system comes about is a complex matter that cannot be discussed here (see Sartori, 1968a, pp. 288–97). Let me simply note that the voter cannot identify himself with an abstract party image until the image is provided, that is to say, as long as he is confronted with mere parties of notabilities. By the same token, and concurrently, the voter cannot perceive the party as an abstract entity unless he acquires a capacity for abstraction, and this implies, in turn, literacy. Under conditions of widespread illiteracy the structural consolidation of a party system can hardly occur. Concretely and simply put, we 'see' a structured party system when the organizational mass party displaces and largely replaces the parties of notables.[15]

The problem at hand can now be restated as follows: plurality systems have no influence (beyond the district) until the party system becomes structured in coincidence with, or in reaction to, the appearance of mass parties. The important implication is that we have long been misled, in this connection, by citing evidence that bears no proof. The authors who deny the reductive effects of plurality systems almost invariably make reference to unstructured party systems, thereby challenging a 'law' in situations in which the law does not apply.[16]

A last point needs clarification. With reference to the contention that plurality systems tend to produce two-party systems, how are such systems to be defined? Remember, a law is worthless if its predicted effect is inadequately specified. And to this end Duverger's hazy notion of 'party dualism' will not do. When is two really two? Here my counting rules (conceived for multipartism in general) require some finessing.

Let us start with listing the standard countries generally classified as two-party countries, namely, the United States, England, New Zealand, Australia, and Canada.[17] Among these countries only the United States does not consistently display sizeable electoral 'third parties'. England has a Liberal third party (variously recombined and redenominated) whose turnout ranges between 10 to as much as 25 percent of the total vote. New Zealand is generally considered a pure two-party case, and yet has had, for over thirty years, a Social Credit party in the 6–20 percent range of returns. Australia is admittedly anomalous, in that one party of its alleged two-party system is in fact a symbiosis of the Liberal and Country parties. However, in the three aforesaid countries 'third parties' obtain votes but hardly ever seats; and if they do, as in England, their parliamentary representation still remains too small to hurt. But Canada definitely has one and eventually two 'third parties' that achieve a parliamentary representation that often turns Canadian cabinets into minority governments.[18] On the face of the above, why is Australia different from Germany's three-party format? And why on earth is Canada generally considered two-party?

In order to reply we must distinguish between the format and the mechanics (or functional characteristics) of two-partism and recognize that the specimen cannot be defined on the basis of the sheer number of its parties (Sartori, 1976, pp. 185–92). In my understanding – and going beyond the format – a two-party *system* is characterized by three traits: (i) over time two parties recurrently and largely outdistance all the others, in such a way that (ii) each of them is in a position to compete for the absolute majority of seats and may thus reasonably expect to alternate in power; and (iii) each of them governs, when in government, alone. On this definition, however, Australia and Canada still do not qualify. In order to include the two countries, as the *consensus scholarum* seemingly demands, the second and third characterizations must be relaxed as follows: the winner who fails to attain a majority of seats opts for minority single-party government instead of yielding to coalition government (Canada), and a standing coalescence of two parties (as in Australia) is considered equivalent to, and counted as, one party.

To be sure, and once again, it must be borne in mind that the above applies to parliamentary systems (presidential systems require a separate treatment). Also, our interest here is on the format, not on the mechanics, not on the full-fledged set of systemic and functional characteristics, of two-partism.

Let it be stipulated, then, that a two-party *format* is defined by *two relevant parties* each of which governs alone (not in coalition), regardless of third parties. The stipulation drops the alternation requirement (as qualified above), and thus permits the inclusion in the category of Ireland. However, Ireland performs with STV, the single transferable vote, which is indeed a pure proportional system. And there are additional countries that are, or have been, two-party with PR: Malta and Austria. Even if one leaves aside, as I do for the time being, the PR based, two-party presidential systems in Latin America, even so it already appears that it cannot be simply held that plurality systems cause (tend to cause) two-partism, or even that the correlation between them is a strong one.

3.4   THE 'LAWS'

We are now ready for the question: Can the influence of electoral systems be generalized in law-like form? Let me try out first a set of largely descriptive rules.[19]

Rule 1. A plurality system cannot produce by itself a nationwide two-party format (as defined), but under all circumstances it will help *maintain* an already existing one. Hence, whenever a two-party format is established, a plurality system exerts a brakelike influence and obtains a freezing effect.

Rule 2. A plurality system will *produce*, in the long run, a two-party format (not the eternalization of the same parties, however) under two conditions: first, when the party system is structured and, second, if the electorate which is refractory to whatever pressure of the electoral system happens to be dispersed in below-plurality proportions throughout the constituencies.

Rule 3. Conversely, a two-party format is *impossible* – under whatever electoral system – if racial, linguistic, ideologically alienated, single-issue, or otherwise incoercible minorities (which cannot be represented by two major mass parties) are concentrated in above-plurality proportions in particular constituencies or geographical pockets. If so, the effect of a plurality system will only be reductive *vis-à-vis* the third parties which do not represent incoercible minorities.

Rule 4. Finally, PR systems also obtain *reductive effects* – though to a lesser and less predictable extent – in proportion to their non-proportionality; and particularly whenever they apply to small-sized constituencies, establish a threshold of representation, or attribute a premium. Under these conditions PR, too, will eliminate the lesser parties whose electorate is dispersed throughout the constituencies; but even a highly impure PR will not eliminate the small parties that dispose of concentrated above-quota strongholds.

It will be noted that my rules largely hinge upon the distribution of electorates. The distribution of partisan allegiances is a historical given, however, only prior to the advent of a structured party system. Since my rules apply after the stage of local fragmentation of politics – under the condition that national mass parties are established – I am concerned only with that distribution of allegiances which remains unaffected by the structural consolidation. Hence my emphasis is on whether or not incoercible *above plurality* or, as the case may be, *above quotient* minorities happen to be geographically concentrated or dispersed.

It should also be noted that Rule 2 already suffices to dispose of India as an exception, because India does not satisfy the condition of being a structured party system.[20] As for Rule 3, it applies nicely to the Canadian case, that is, the rule accounts for the fact that Canada displays, despite plurality, a three-four party format. Rule 3 is also well confirmed by the experience of Sri Lanka between 1948 and 1977: for at the 1977 last plurality election all the minor parties, except for the regionally concentrated ethnic Tamil parties, had disappeared.[21] Finally, Rule 4 applies nicely to Ireland and Japan (with small 3-to-5 member constituencies), to Greece, Spain and Austria (which also display relatively small constituencies of, respectively, 5, 6 and 7 members),[22] and also helps explain (on account of the exclusion clause) the format of the German Federal Republic.[23]

The next step is to relate the formats predicted by the foregoing four rules to *systemic characteristics*, that is, to distinctive types of party systems. From the typology that I have developed at length elsewhere (Sartori, 1976, pp. 125-216, 273-93), let me derive three major systemic patterns: (1) *two-party mechanics*, i.e., bipolar single-party alternation in government; (2) *moderate multipartism*, i.e., bipolar shifts among coalition governments; (3) *polarized multipartism*, i.e., systems characterized by multipolar competition, center-located coalitions with peripheral turnover, and anti-system parties. In this typology the decisive variable is systemic *polarization,* defined as the distance (ideological or other) between the most distant relevant parties.[24] The question now is: Will the format be followed by the expected, corresponding mechanics (functional properties)? Given structural consolidation (necessary condition) and polarization as the intervening and, to some extent, dependent variable, I hypothesize as follows:

Hypothesis 1. When the single-member plurality formula produces a two-party format (Rules 1 and 2), the format will in turn produce a two-party mechanics if, and only if, the polarization of the polity is low. With high polarization, two-party mechanics breaks down. However, since a two-party mechanics implies centripetal competition, it tends to lessen, rather than heighten, systemic polarization.

Hypothesis 2. Assuming a below-quota dispersion of the incoercible minorities (if any), impure PR formulas are likely to allow for one-two additional parties above the two-party format, that is, three-four parties. This format will in turn engender the mechanics of moderate multipartism if, and only if, the polity does not display high polarization. However, since moderate multipartism still is bipolar-converging (centripetal competition), it will not tend to increase systemic polarization.

Hypothesis 3. Relatively pure or pure PR systems easily allow for a five- to seven-party format. Even so, under conditions of medium–low polarization, the coalitional mechanics of moderate multipartism is not impeded. However, under conditions of high polarization the format will display the mechanical characteristics of polarized multipartism, thereby including a multipolar competition that eventually heightens systemic polarization.

The above is so condensed as to be only of suggestive value – and I shall have to leave it at that.[25] For I have yet to complete the argument. Thus far the independent (causal) variable has been the electoral system. But we already know that another independent variable has to be accounted for: *the party system qua system of channelment.* Let us attend, then, to assessing the case in its entirety as in Table 3.1, which displays four possible combinations: (I) strong electoral system and strong party system, (II) feeble electoral system and strong

Table 3.1 Combined influences of party and electoral systems

	Electoral systems	
Party systems	*Strong*	*Feeble*
	(I)	(II)
Strong (structured)	Reductive effect of electoral system	Countervailing-blocking effect of party system
	(III)	(IV)
Feeble (unstructured)	Restraining-reductive constituency effect	No influence

party system, (III) strong electoral system and feeble party system, and (IV) feeble electoral system and feeble party system. Since the dichotomous reduction squeezes out the intermediate possibilities, it should be understood that the 'strong electoral systems' include not only, as is obvious, the plurality formula but also the strongly impure PR formulas (in substance, all the cases covered by my initial rules). Conversely, the 'feeble electoral systems' refer to the relatively pure to pure PR formulas (mathematically and districtwise).

Combination I requires no further explanation. All the plurality based two-party systems singled out earlier fall here, thus confirming the predicted *reductive effect*. India, on the other hand, falls into Combination III, and therefore no longer stands as a major and crippling exception to the first law of Duverger.

Combination II indicates that, when PR (even feeble PR) encounters a structured party system, the voter is still *restrained*, though not by the electoral system but by the potency of party channelment. In this case, then, the electoral system is counteracted by the party system: we have, I say, a *blocking* or a *countervailing effect*. That is the same as saying that here the causal factor, the independent variable, is the party system. Combination II not only explains why the introduction of PR may not be followed by 'more parties' but may even allow for two-party systems (Malta, and Austria between 1966–83) and/or formats (Ireland). The combination disposes, then, of the exceptions: two-partism without plurality. The general argument is this: a particularly strong structuring of the party system replaces (as sufficient condition two) the manipulative impact of a strong electoral system (sufficient condition one).

Combination III indicates that, when a strong electoral system encounters an unstructured party system, the effect is only a *constituency effect*, and specifically a restraining effect on the voter that translates itself into a reductive effect on the constituency parties. Here, then, the electoral system cannot obtain reductive effects on the national scale. Still, the constituency impact remains, thereby discouraging fickleness and encouraging two-person races at the district level. The combination illustrates the state of affairs in much of continental Europe until or around World War I, and equally explains the current failure of plurality systems (e.g. in Poland for the Senate) to reduce fragmentation.

Combination IV indicates *no influence*, meaning that, when relatively pure PR is combined with structurelessness, neither the electoral nor the party systems intervene in the political process with a manipulative impact of their own. Here the general point is that the more we approach pure PR, and the more electoral or related obstacles are removed, the less whatever party system happens to exist is 'caused' by the electoral system. Much of Latin America, on account of the intermittence of its party experience, i.e., of the repeated interruptions (detrimental to consolidation) caused by military seizures, comes close to falling into this cluster. And the combination conveys that the newborn countries and the former communist states that start with PR have set for themselves the least favorable conditions for overcoming party atomization and for attaining structural consolidation.

We can now finally outline rules that qualify as being laws formulated in terms of necessary and sufficient conditions. Since the electoral system is the causal factor under investigation, the electoral system is assumed to be *a sufficient condition* and, more precisely, the pertinent, albeit *not the exclusive* sufficient condition. As for the *necessary conditions*, our inquiry has found two such conditions, namely: (i) systemic structuring (of the party system), as opposed to structurelessness; (ii) sizeable above-plurality concentrations or, with PR, sizeable above-quota concentrations, as opposed to below-plurality or below-quota distributions (of the first preferences of the voters) hereinafter abridged as *cross-constituency dispersion*. On these premises the 'laws' that I venture to propose are as follows:

Law 1 Given systemic structuring and cross-constituency dispersion (as joint necessary conditions), *plurality systems* cause (are a sufficient condition of) a two-party format.

  1.1 Alternatively, a particularly strong systemic structuring is, alone, the necessary substitutive sufficient condition for causing a two-party format.

Law 2 Given systemic structuring but failing cross-constituency dispersion, *plurality systems* cause (are a sufficient condition of) the elimination of below-plurality parties but cannot eliminate, and thus permit, as many parties above two as are permitted by sizeable above-plurality concentrations.

Law 3 Given systemic structuring, *proportional representation* obtains a reductive effect caused (as a sufficient condition) by its nonproportionality. Hence, the greater the impurity of PR, the higher the entry costs for the smaller parties, and the stronger the reductive effect; and, conversely, the lesser the impurity, the feebler the reductive effect.

  3.1 Alternatively, a particularly strong systemic structuring is alone the necessary and sufficient condition for maintaining whatever party format preexisted the introduction of PR.

Law 4 Failing systemic structuring and assuming pure (close to pure) PR, that is, an equal (quasi-equal) cost of entry for all, the number of parties is free to become as large as the quota permits.

The above numbering may cause some confusion. How many laws do we have? At most, four, since laws 1.1 and 3.1

simply allow for the incorporation and/or dismissal of apparent exceptions under the proviso: varying the condition, the same effect may follow, because one sufficient condition is substituted by another. In fact, the 'true' laws (if true) are three, since Law 4 simply establishes where the effects of electoral systems end. So, the requirement of parsimony is surely met. On the other hand, the objection might be that my laws are too abstract and not specific enough. Not so, provided that they are read – as they are supposed to be read – in conjunction with the four rules set forth earlier. In particular, the specifics of Law 1 are given in Rules 1 and 2; the specifics of Law 2 are provided by Rule 3, and the specifics of Law 3 are supplied by Rule 4.

As the foregoing discussion shows, the much recalled 'multiplying effect' of PR is nowhere to be found. The logical point is this: since PR is supposed to mirror 'in proportion,' how can it multiply? What strange kind of mirror is that? I submit that the multiplying effect of PR is an optical illusion prompted by the historical sequencing of electoral systems. The first PR country was Belgium (1899), followed by Sweden (1907). Elsewhere PR generally appeared in the wake of World War I, and in the prewar European countries of the time PR was invariably preceded by plurality or, more often, by double-ballot formulas that equally displayed plurality-type restraining effects. It should also be recalled that the introduction of PR was often accompanied by enfranchisements, by the entry into politics of hitherto excluded lower-class voters who generally sought new parties, 'their own' parties. Thus, when PR was introduced it did result in a roundabout *removal of obstacles*; previous voters were allowed a greater freedom of expressing their first preferences, and new voters the very freedom of voting. So, when we say that PR multiplies the number of parties, we forget to complete the sentence by saying: with respect to a state of affairs in which the number of parties was kept small by small electorates and/or reduced by 'strong' electoral formulas. And when this qualification is entered, the optical illusion disappears.

The correct argument is, thus, that whenever the introduction of PR happens to be followed by the surge of new relevant parties, we are not really pointing at the *effects* of PR but at the *side-effects* resulting from the removal of preexisting obstacles. Had the historical sequencing been from PR to plurality, it would hardly have occurred to us that PR 'causes' party system fragmentation. Certainly, the more PR mirrors, the less it penalizes and obstructs the surge of new parties or the splitting of existing parties. But freedom to surge is no more the cause of surging than freedom to eat is the cause of eating. The alleged multiplying effect of PR is, at best, an *indirect* effect and, by the same token, an *uncertain* effect. Thus, there is no puzzle in the fact that the introduction of PR *may not* produce more parties.

To recapitulate, pure PR is a *no-effect* electoral system.[26] Conversely, PR affects the party system to the extent that it is *non-proportional*, and this on a variety of counts: the relatively small size of the constituencies, clauses of exclusion, majority premiums and, lastly, disproportional translations of the votes into seats. It follows from this that whenever PR obtains manipulative effects, these effects are restrictive, not multiplicative. Hence, the influence of PR merely represents and enfeeblement of the same influence that is exerted by the majority-plurality systems.

Up to now I have not entered into the picture the double ballot – even though I have indicated (*supra* 1.5) that it is an important system in its own right. The reason for having left the double ballot to last is that it can either be given majoritarian or proportional formulations. In the first case the double ballot obtains the standard majoritarian reductive effect on the number of parties (though a somewhat enfeebled one); but this decapitation is obtained in a far gentler manner, that is to say, with far lesser manipulative-coercive pressure on the voter. In the second case – which makes sense, in practice, for three-four member constituencies at most – the double ballot system performs as a proportional system that disproportionately favors some parties over others. But the pliability of the double ballot allows for so many variations that before trying to codify their effects in law form we must provide (in the next chapter) a descriptive account of the range of possibilities of the various double ballot schemes.

It is apparent that I have been building cumulatively on the premises of Duverger. And since Taagepera and Shugart equally come up with a reformulation of 'Duverger's expressions . . . into a single rule' that they call the 'generalized Duverger's rule', by way of conclusion let us compare the mileages respectively afforded by the two routes. Taagepera's and Shugart's generalized Duverger's rule reads as follows: 'The effective number of electoral parties is usually within ±1 unit from $N = 1.25 \, (2 + \log M)$' (1989, p. 145). The parsimony of their unified rule is beautifully pleasing. However, does it amount to an *explanatory law*? While the authors ask themselves, 'Is the new rule on the number of parties a law, a hypothesis, or an empirical data fit?', their reply is that 'for practical purposes, it really does not matter' (*ibid.*). But this is an all too easy way out. For one, and on their own recognition (see pp. 146–55), the empirical fit of the rule is poor. For instance, 'countries such as India among plurality systems and Finland and Switzerland among PR systems, have numbers of parties higher than expected. Countries with either fewer parties than expected based on their issue dimensions (Italy), or with few issue dimensions in spite of PR (Austria) result in lower than expected number of parties' (p. 155). So, India, Finland, Switzerland, Italy, Austria are out of fit in the Taagepera–Shugart generalized rule, while they all fit in my laws. And then, what is the explanatory power for their 'single quantitative expression for Duverger's rule'? What exactly causes exactly what? All in all, it seems to me that the quantitative rendering of Duverger obtains little more, or little else, than a very loose 'frequency law' that strongly impoverishes, among other things, the information that my approach instead supplies.

NOTES

1. The fact that the new, 1993 Italian electoral laws retain a 25 percent of proportional representation (for both Houses)

mitigates but does not alter the truly revolutionary nature of the reform. And the fact that the reform was triggered by a referendum still leaves the Italian changes as a case of peaceful and free self-reform.

2. This is my translation, for the standard one in English by the Norths (1953) from the first edition of *Les Partis Politiques* (1951) is imprecise and misleading. For a fuller account and criticism of Duverger, see Sartori, 1986, pp. 43–45.

3. For the purpose at hand I leave aside Duverger's assimilation – in the second law – between double ballot and PR, which is plainly incorrect. Duverger himself, in an earlier formulation, separated the two cases as follows: '(1) PR tends to a system of multiple, *rigid* and independent parties, (2) the double ballot plurality system tends to multiple, *flexible* and independent parties' (Duverger et al., 1950, p. 13. My emphasis). This is more accurate, though still unsatisfactory. It should be borne in mind, however, that Duverger accounted, at the time, only for the experience of the French III Republic.

4. This applies also to the authors that share Duverger's law-seeking interest, namely, Rae (1971) and Riker (1982). More exactly, Rae does not build upon Duverger and proposes an approach of his own, while Riker's amendments to Duverger simply make matter worse. See, for a critical appraisal of both authors, Sartori, 1986, pp. 45–48.

5. In addition to the two collective volumes edited by Lijphart and Grofman (1984 and 1986), reference is especially made to Katz (1980), whose main focus is on intraparty competition, and to Taagepera and Shugart (1989), which is a sophisticated quantitative-mathematical work.

6. In what follows I largely draw from my chapter in Grofman and Lijphart (1986), pp. 43–68, where I partially draw, in turn, from an early writing of mine published in 1968 (see Bibliography) but circulated as a paper in 1966.

7. This means that given the cause C, the effect E remains undetermined and cannot be surely known *ex ante*. However, a causal assumption is still justified in that we do know, first, that some effect will almost surely follow and, second, that a given effect is far more likely than any other. For a more detailed explanation see Sartori, *La Politica*, 1979, pp. 52–54. See also Sartori 1986, pp. 49-51.

8. Electoral systems also have, to be sure, indirect and distal effects. But on these later.

9.   'Electoral Reform', *The Economist*, May 1, 1993, p. 24.
10. The full argument is in Sartori, 1976, pp. 119–25 and 300–19.
11. Earlier tries at measuring both number and size of parties are by Lijphart and Blondel, illustrated and criticized in Sartori, 1976, pp. 304–06.
12. I spell out in greater detail the feebleness and limitations of Rae's index of fractionalization in Sartori, 1976, pp. 307–15.
13. However, the value of this information is overvalued. To my mind discontinuous size thresholds are far more important than continuous relative sizes. I distinguish, therefore, between predominant (absolute majority) and dominant (relative majority) parties, and thereafter look into the intervals that separate one party from another in their respective parliamentary strength. See Sartori, 1976, pp. 192–201.
14. To be sure, strong–feeble dichotomizes a continuum that can be rendered (see Sartori, 1968b) by finer slicings. Nohlen observes that this distinction rests on 'normative premises' (1984a, p. 85); but I am afraid that I miss his point.
15. The structuring of party systems in Western Europe largely corresponds to what Lipset and Rokkan called their 'freezing' (1967). This freezing appeared to reverse its course into a defreezing between the middle of the Sixties and the middle of the Seventies; but the greater volatility of that decade was successfully counteracted by the traditional parties. The Nineties seemingly attest to a new defreezing and, this time, to a deeper one. At the time of this writing many structured party systems appear to have entered a process of 'destructuring' – but not to the point of affecting my definition.
16. This generally applies to the nineteenth century experience with plurality and double-ballot elections. It equally applies, however, to the current experience of Poland, where the October 1991 plurality election to the Senate produced – as my argument assumes – just about as much fragmentation as the PR election to the low chamber, the Seym. (Both chambers were dissolved in May 1993; but the new electoral law remains unchanged for the Senate.)
17. While these standard cases all abide by plurality elections, still Duverger was quite wrong in asserting that 'nowhere in the world has PR produced or maintained two-partism' (1954, p. 276). As we are about to see, two-party formats (and even systems) are quite possible with PR. However, the preliminary caveat is that two-partism in parliamentary systems differs from

two-partism in presidential systems. On this account I leave out of the picture, for the time being, the presidential Latin American countries, such as Argentina, Costa Rica and Venezuela, that surely display a two-party format (Colombia and Uruguay are highly dubious cases), and also postpone the analysis of the United States.

18. Canada's leading party has been, since 1896, the Liberal party, with the Conservative party coming second as the relevant party of the system. However, the CCF – a social-democratic party renamed in 1965 the New Democratic Party, NDP – has consistently managed to win enough seats (from a minimum of 6.1 to a maximum of 11.3 percent in 1980) to disturb a single-party absolute majority. Furthermore, in the past the Social Credit party equally managed to win, if only intermittently, sizeable access to representation (up to almost 12 percent in 1962 and 1963). These configurations are radically altered by the October 1993 election, in which two new parties have emerged with a consistent share of seats (each in the 18 percent range): the 'Quebec Bloc' and the 'Reform Party'. Even so the pattern remains, as in the past, that a two-party format is never obtained.

19. In this section I repeat with no change the rules and laws set forth in Sartori, 1986, pp. 58–64. To restate a rule amounts to altering it; and I have no reason thus far to do that.

20. India's party system might at most be classified as 'semistructured' on account of the fact that only one of its parties, the Congress party (founded in 1885 and thus, long prior to independence, *the* party of non-Moslem Indians), has attained the degree of structural consolidation attainable in a country in which illiteracy still looms as large as it does across more than 850 million inhabitants. Even so, 'personality politics' still predominates, as attested by the massive swings of the late 70s: the dramatic downslide of the Congress party in 1977 (down to 28% of the seats, from a previous 68%) followed by another landslide victory in 1980. India certainly attests, on the other hand, to what a plurality system impedes. Were India to switch to PR, it is a safe conjecture that it would quickly become one of the most fragmented of all known party systems.

21. More exactly, in Sri Lanka the nonethnic minor parties and the independents fell from 26 seats obtained in 1960 to 2 seats in 1970 and in 1977; while the two Marxist parties (Communists and LLSP) fell from the 25 seats still obtained in 1970 to no

seats in 1977. Unfortunately for our purposes, the 1978 constitution dropped the plurality system.

22. These are rounded averages which pose no problem with one-digit values. However, as the size grows the average (and even the median) district magnitude can be a very misleading measure unless the dispersion is controlled. Fisichella's (1982, pp. 251–52) index of variability attributes the smallest dispersion (0.81) to Ireland, and the widest dispersion (11.77) to Argentina, whose constituencies range from a 2-member to the 50-member size of Buenos Aires. Brazil has a similar dispersion, with constituencies ranging between 60- and 8-member magnitudes. Let it also be noted that Rae's computations for district magnitudes are, in part, flawed. As correctly pointed out by Lijphart (1985, p. 9), 'in PR systems that have two levels of districts. . .Rae simply counts the total number of districts at both levels. This is a serious error: it yields relatively small district magnitudes, whereas the effect of the . . . higher level of districts is to make the lower-level districts larger'.

23. Remember, however, that the German 5 percent *Sperrklause* is not the only, and not even the major, reason for its three-party format (*supra* 2.2).

24. Concerning 'polarization,' see esp. Sani and Sartori (1983) for how the concept is defined, measured, and fares with the comparative evidence.

25. Other, and better known, correspondences and implications bear on how plurality and PR systems, respectively, affect governability and the very principle of representation. But on these topics later.

26. To be sure 'no effect' on the number of parties, which is the dependent variable under consideration. For, surely, PR has effects in other domains and, in general, electoral systems always are of consequence on something.

4 Choosing an Electoral System

4.1 ASSESSING MAJORITARIANISM

As regards the translation between votes and seats electoral systems can be considered continuous, since the major variable is here the constituency size, and given the fact that sizes that range continuously (serially) from 1 to about 40–50 all exist in some country or another. But as regards their ends and their underlying reason for being, I insist that electoral systems must be neatly disjoined into majoritarian and proportional. The alternative may be stated as follows: 'Representational systems belong to two main patterns . . . The English type sacrifices the representativeness of parliament to the need of efficient government, while the French type sacrifices efficient government to the representativeness of parliament . . . [And] we cannot build a representational system that maximizes at onc and the same time the function of functioning and the function of mirroring.'[1]

Before entering this discussion let it be remembered that majoritarian systems need not be plurality systems (e.g., the alternative vote calls for an absolute majority), nor singlemember district systems (for a single winner with list voting is a conceivable possibility, and has been the case in Turkey in the Fifties). And while the plurality criterion is by far the most employed one, it should be well understood that we are in fact dealing with different majority levels which are often mixed up – also because they are confusingly labeled. To wit, we first encounter the 'qualified majority', which is required to be a higher than 51 percent majority (generally between the 55–65 percent levels), followed by the 'absolute majority', which is obtained by just passing the 50 percent threshold. This absolute majority is also called 'simple majority' (in contrast to the qualified majority). What next?

53

Well, we generally say that what comes next is the 'relative majority', which is the same as 'plurality'. Yes and no, however. For majorities move up and down, depending on their base line, which can either be the universe of all those who are entitled to vote, i.e., the electorate on record, or the actual number of the actual voters (whose votes are valid). In this reference the absolute majority is (properly speaking) the simple majority of the electorate, while the simple majority of the voters is (properly speaking) a relative majority. A plurality is, instead, 'whatever majority', and far more often than not consists of the 'largest minority'. But for all practical intents and purposes, let us leave aside the fine points, and let us go along with the loose stipulation that plurality is the same as relative majority.

I was saying that the English theory and practice of representation sacrifices the representativeness of parliament to the need of efficient government. Indeed, first-past-the-post electoral systems seek effective government by manufacturing governing-supporting majorities. Indeed, majoritarian systems pay no heed to 'exact representation', favor the overrepresentation of the stronger contestants and make no bones about severely underrepresenting the feebler ones. The disrepresentative distortion may go as far as allowing that a party wins the government (the absolute majority of seats) while finishing second in the popular vote.[2] And this is, for the critics of majoritarianism, its insurmountable fault.

Its defenders often argue that in many cases the difference in proportionality between plurality and PR outcomes is quite limited.[3] For instance, in the United States the single member district system does represent in proportion, more or less, the Democratic and Republican parties. True, but a third party that enters the fray immediately discovers another truth, namely, how crushingly disrepresentative the plurality system turns out to be in its disfavor.[4] And the point is that the argument is misconstrued. The finding that plurality elections do not necessarily lead to unfair representation closes the stable doors when the horses have already escaped. That is to say that the argument looks at returns that discount the very effect of the electoral system, namely, that voters have practiced 'strategic voting' and that third parties have been eliminated. The point is, then, that the more majoritarian systems 'work' (as intended), the more their manipulative impact disappears from our findings, that is, from the statistics that correlate votes with seats. So, the charge that plurality elections obstruct and distort 'exact representation' is sustained and stands.

Having conceded, as we should, this demerit, the issue turns on the merits. Majoritarian systems are generally upheld on four grounds or counts: first, that they elect (help elect) a governing majority and, by this route, a government; second, that they reduce party fragmentation, eventually to only two parties; third, that they create a direct (more direct) relationship between electors and their representative; fourth, that they improve the quality of the elected office holders.

The first merit – electing a government – obtains only when it obtains, that is, only when majoritarian elections produce a two-party system; and this is established by our previously outlined (*supra*, 3.4) Rules 1 and 2, by Hypothesis 1, and by Law number 1. If the claim is made when the conditions that allow for it are absent, then it is an unwarranted claim. So, the strongest argument in favor of plurality elections is also a strongly 'conditioned' argument, and becomes a false argument whenever the party system is insufficiently structured and whenever incoercible electorates are insufficiently dispersed (in below-plurality proportions) across the constituencies.[5] On the other hand – and other conditions being equal – it is generally true that a plurality system is more conducive to effective government than a PR system. But this is a diluted governability claim; and a claim that cannot be pushed any further than that.

The second merit – reducing party fragmentation – is the more generally sustainable one. The reductive effect of plurality elections is established by my Rule 3 and Law number 2. So, while the first-past-the-post system cannot, on its own, reduce the number of parties to the two-party format, even so it very often compresses or keeps their number at relatively low levels. And even when this compression is not readily apparent in an enormous, and enormously diverse country such as India (and possibly, in the future, China), it still is the case that under a proportional arrangement India-like countries would probably lapse and collapse into pulverization.

The third alleged merit of plurality elections is that they bring about a direct linkage between the elector and its elected representative. This linkage cannot be disputed in principle, for in the single-member district system there is no place for the intermediation of party lists and therefore – almost by definition – the relation between voting and electing is a direct one. In practice, however, the import of this directness is very much open to doubt. For one, any relationship that claims a direct significance must account for the numbers that are involved. Constituency magnitudes vary enormously. Small countries can afford 1 member for every 20,000 voters (New Zealand); but medium-sized countries generally require some 50,000 voters (UK) per MP; and large countries (from the U.S. to India's maximum) contain single-member districts with hundreds of thousands of voters. Assuming, for illustrative purposes, the ratio of 50,000 electors per 1 elected, in this instance my vote counts for one fifty-thousandth. Does this ratio establish a meaningful linkage? Secondly, the first-past-the-post winner takes all with 50 percent or more of the vote only if the race is confined to only two runners; and since this is seldom the case, the front runner generally wins all with less than 50 percent of the vote. It is often the case, then, that more than 50 percent of the voters simply lose their vote. How about them? If we insist on the directness aspect, by the same token we must admit that a majority of the district voters is all too frequently not represented at all.

The more sensible argument would thus appear to be that the plurality winner represents its district – period. If so, however, 'directness' acquires a different meaning and basically becomes 'proximity', that is to say, locality-centered or, better still, constituency-centered politics. Since this is an important point, I shall come back to it shortly.

The fourth merit – improving the quality of the personnel of politics – encounters the preliminary difficulty that 'quality' is difficult to assess. Insofar as the voter is confronted with bad guys – corrupt, greedy and indeed dirty politicians – then clean, honest and well-meaning politicians surely represent a quality improvement. But kicking the rascals out does not automatically bring in 'good' politicians who are good at their job, that is to say, whose qualities are competency, vision, and leadership capabilities. Good people are not, by any necessity, the cure for bad government, for private and public virtues are not of the same order.

Having recognized that 'quality selection' is an elusive matter, it should also be acknowledged that with plurality single-member elections the personal qualities and traits of the candidates running for office acquire a greater salience than with PR list systems. Yet, does 'person voting' really make a difference with regard to who is chosen as a candidate for office? The answer to this question is – we have seen *supra*, 2.1 – that the personality of the candidate matters and does make a difference in the unsafe constituencies, but hardly in the safe ones. Where the race is close and the electorate volatile, parties or political machines are prompted to look around for the most electorally attractive candidate they can find. But in their safe constituencies parties can afford to propose, and do impose, their own personnel regardless of quality considerations.

Now the point that plurality elections are, or may be, conducive to localism and constituency-centered politics. This development is encouraged by the 'direct democracy' democrat, for it does bring politics close to the people. It is also taken very much for granted in the United States, where it has become commonplace to assert that 'all politics is local politics'. Yet, if all politics is local, how can national politics be decently managed? Since a presidential system can cope with centrifugal and localistic pulls better than a parliamentary one, Americans still fail to perceive how much trouble looms ahead for their system of government as congressional politics increasingly breaks down into a constituency-serving 'retail politics'. But whether naive democrats and Americans realize it or not, the question is a formidable on: if all politics is local, what happens to the polity as a whole, to the common interest and to the common good?

Remember, the core justification of majoritarian systems is that they promote governability by containing and reducing party fragmentation. Now, if party fragmentation is an ill, by the same token district-based and district-dispersed fragmentation must be seen as a far greater and more devastating ill. And it would certainly be a supreme irony if the electoral system intended as a means of efficient government reversed itself into the very killer of any possible good governing.

The issue thus becomes whether the localistic development of the single-member district system is somewhat 'natural' and inevitable, or can instead by resisted. As we look around we find that the American path has yet to be followed in the other English-speaking plurality countries. And the reason for this difference is not hard to seek. While a presidential system based on the division of power is somewhat sheltered *vis-à-vis* an erratic and localistic behavior of its MPs, this is no longer the case with parliamentary systems, and especially with two-party ones. As we know, the *sine qua non* condition of a two-party polity is a structured (strong) nation-wide party system; and this implies that district-centered politics and a two-party polity are incompatibles: if localism affirms itself, a two-party state purely and simply breaks down. In England and in the Commonwealth countries localism is resisted and counter-acted, then, by the strength and the very self-preserving logic of the party system. The plurality nurturing of localistic-driven politics might well remain confined, therefore, to the United States. But in the face of a growing, generalized party enfeeblement, the last on narrow-minded 'common-disinter-est' politics has yet to be seen.

4.2 ASSESSING PROPORTIONALISM

Proportional representation embodies and pushes forward one overriding concern: the equal allocation 'in proportion' of votes into seats. Its undisputed merit thus is fairness in representa-tion. And for most people this is a winning claim. Nevertheless PR calls for two major, related criticisms: first, that it produces (or, more exactly, allows for) excessive party fragmentation and, second, that it is insensitive to, or copes badly with, the governability requirement, the need for effective governance.

The fragmentation indictment can be disposed of quickly, since the extent of its validity has already been established (*supra*, 3.4) by my Rule 4, Hypotheses 2 and 3, and Laws number 3 and 4. Their gist is, remember, that the greater the impurity of PR, the lesser the parties. Thus many impure PR systems keep the number of their 'relevant parties' down to 3–4, at most 5; and this is not, in and by itself, a particularly damaging degree of fragmentation. True, most of the 3-to-5 party systems that I call of moderate pluralism (Sartori, 1976, pp. 173–85) require coalition governments.[6] But before coming to this point, let the one at hand be settled as follows: that the fragmentation of the party system resulting from pure or quasi-pure PR does become a problem with extreme pluralism (more-than-five parties), and even more so in conjunction with polarization. The fragmentation indictment eminently applies or applied, therefore, to France (IV Republic), Italy (under the PR system of 1948–93), Israel and, to be sure, to countries like present-day Poland.[7] Here the problem was or is a serious one, but arises from excessively pure PR and can be remedied in its own terms by adopting an impure form of PR.

The second charge, namely, that PR fails to cope with governability, requires instead some probing. Certainly, with PR the representational process becomes a neatly divided two-step process in which the voters only elect a parliament, and the parliamentary body subsequently and independently decides, on its own grounds, who shall govern, for how long.[8] It is also the case, as was just noted, that with PR most governments turn out to be coalition governments. But do coalitions necessarily make for 'inferior' government? Are coalition governments necessarily under-performers *vis-à-vis* single-party government? The issue has three sides: (i) the longevity or stability of governments, (ii) the assignment of responsibility, and (iii) whether coalitions can really govern. The first point will be looked into in due course (*infra* 6.6). The second one can be left here at conceding that with coalition governments who is to blame, that is, who is responsible for doing, or not doing what, easily defies pinpointing. However, the crucial point is the third one, namely, whether coalition governments are generally conducive to ineffective, or incoherent, or gridlocked government. And here the answer is: It depends.

Firstly, it depends on how many are the coalition partners. For instance, coalitions of two parties can be expected to be easier to manage than, say, coalitions among five parties. Secondly, and more importantly, it depends on whether coalitions are (regardless of how many parties enter them) coalescent or conflictual, on whether their component units play in harmony or instead play against each other. And to this effect the crucial variable is the overall polarization of the political system.

Polarization boils down to being a 'distance' – either of the ideological left-right kind, or of some other variety. Thus in a polarized polity voters and parties are aliens among themselves, are distant from each other, and this implies that it is both difficult and electorally unrewarding for them to agree on just about anything. Under these conditions coalitions are *heterogeneous,* and by the same token uncooperative, litigious and stalemate-prone. Conversely, in a relatively non-polarized polity (characterized, therefore, by a pragmatic orientation to politics) voters and parties are largely unprincipled, relatively close to each other, and can therefore easily strike bargains and agree on compromises. Under these conditions coalitions are *homogeneous,* and by the same token capable of playing a cooperative game.[9]

Proportional representation does not *necessarily* lead, then, to quarrelsome and stalemated coalition government. As with the fragmentation charge, the ungovernability charge does not apply to PR unqualifiedly. It surely applies, however, when PR brings about heterogeneous coalitions between partners or, indeed, non-partners that play a veto game against each other. And when this is the case PR deserves all the criticism it gets.

In spite of the aforesaid drawbacks, it should be remembered that when PR was enacted at the end of the last century it came as a most useful, and indeed indispensable, means for the progressive integration of the anti-system, externally created parties (basically, socialist and Catholic parties) into the liberal-democratic order.[10] The common notion is that PR was first introduced in Belgium in order to save the Liberal party from the kind of extinction that happened later to the English Liberal party. Yes; but the unintended benefits soon became far greater – across continental Europe – than the contingent interest of saving the pre-enfranchisement nineteenth-century parties of opinion and/or of notables. The unforeseen benefit was that coalition government permitted the access to government of the socialist parties, and by this route their gradual, de facto acceptance (despite their revolutionary marxist doctrine) of the bourgeois state. Especially in the 1920s an all-socialist government would have been a very unpalatable and risky experiment, whereas a socialist sharing of power in coalition with the moderate parties lessened the fear and appeared acceptable. It is true, as I have conceded earlier, that coalition governments obscure responsibility and cover up smoke-shrouded deals. The other side of the coin is, however, that this low visibility always eases – as much today as it did in the past for the externally created parties – the reciprocal 'giving-in' that coalition partnership requires.

There is, then, a lesson in the above, which is that PR and coalition governments may help the 'difficult societies' in muddling through and in hanging together. That is to say that without PR difficult societies might well become 'impossible societies'. We shall comment further on this at the end of the chapter.

4.3 ASSESSING THE DOUBLE BALLOT

The double ballot system has been widely used in the past: with single-member districts in France (during the Second Empire, and subsequently under the Third Republic between 1885–1936), Spain (1870–1931), the Netherlands (1906–18), Germany (1906–19), Austria (1906–19), Norway (1906–21); and with multi-member constituencies in Belgium (until

1900), Norway (until 1906), Italy (between 1882–1891), Switzerland (until 1919), Spain (before 1870 and between 1931 and 1936).[11] The examples indicate that the double ballot has generally existed and performed under conditions of 'no effect', or of minimal effect. While the above recalled countries differed in a number of respects (and Germany and Austria are best set aside as monarchic systems), they generally displayed, at the time, an unstructured or poorly structured party system – and we know that when parties are feeble and largely 'nominal' the electoral system makes little difference (*supra* 3.4).

Thereafter the double ballot system was swept away by PR. The double ballot had to give in, in principle, to the new and seemingly irresistible principle of equal representation; and found no stout defenders because it was PR that allowed for the survival of the traditional parties of notables. Therefore when the effects of electoral systems came under the limelight of scholarship there had been no instance of a double ballot performing within a structured party system. Remember that when Duverger formulated around 1950 his laws, he too was looking at the PR system that had been adopted by the French Fourth Republic. And since the Third Republic had been as fragmented as the Fourth one, it was probably on this basis that Duverger assimilated the double ballot to PR.[12] Subsequent authors have rectified this error and have considered the double ballot a majoritarian system; but they have equally misappraised it. For instance, Richard Rose assimilates the double ballot to the alternative vote as follows:

> The two-ballot plurality system used in the Fifth French Republic is a *variant* on the alternative vote . . . The difference between the Australian and French forms of alternative vote is limited, but of practical political importance. Both systems . . . heavily penalize parties which have a large vote, but more enemies than supporters. Both ask voters to state more than one preference. But the Australian system leaves it to the voter to decide his preference, ordering candidates *all at once* in a single ballot. By contrast the French system also gives an initiative to the candidates

and parties after the results of the first ballot are in. (Rose, 1983, pp. 32–33. My emphasis)

It seems to me that Rose's interpretation is quite blind to what he describes. To begin with, if the double ballot is reduced to just one of its many possibilities – the single-member plurality formula – then we lose sight of the overall mightiness of the system. Indeed, to argue that the double ballot is a variant of the alternative vote is like arguing (I admit to hyperbole) that an eagle is a variant of a fly. That aside, the similarities perceived by Rose are, if anything, dissimilarities. The alternative vote requires an absolute majority. The French parliamentary double ballot requires only a plurality; the former 'orders' the candidates, the latter does not; the former does not allow voters to change their vote, the latter does. These are hardly 'limited' differences. But then, why assimilate the double ballot to something else? In this manner one misses that the system's unique characteristic – that the voter *re-votes* – is also its central characteristic. All other electoral systems are one-shot; the double ballot, and the double ballot only, is a two-shot system. With one shot the voter shoots very much in the dark; with two shots he or she shoots, the second time, in full daylight. But all of this demands a closer look.

At the first round of voting the voter can and does freely express his first preference. His freedom is maximal when there is no threshold (or only a minimal barrier) for the admission of the candidates to the second ballot; and is equally very great with multi-member districts. On the other hand, the calculating voter's freedom is 'less free' when the admission to the run-off is filtered by relatively high thresholds, and especially when only the two front runners are admitted to the second round. These differences notwithstanding, the point remains that the double ballot allows for a voter that can be just as free, in the first round, as he or she is with PR. Note, further, that since the first ballot is a selection, not an election (unless a candidate wins immediately the absolute majority), the first ballot comes close to being a functional equivalent of a *primary voting*: it sorts out the candidates most preferred by most voters. This assimilation should not be overworked. Still the case can be made that the first ballot is like-a-primary without posing any of the problems of the American primary.[13]

Moving on, the second round generally occurs two weeks later on the basis of the voting returns of the first round. And at this stage the voter does become pressured into 'strategic voting' for possible winners. However – and this is the crucial aspect – the voter pressured into voting for his second/third preference (or, at the worst, for the lesser evil) *cannot blame the electoral system* for this constraint; he must blame first and above all the majority will of the other voters: it is *they* who force him. The constraint of the electoral system largely becomes the constraint of actual voting distributions.

And then, why perceive this as a constraint? The theory of voting has deluged us with the notions of 'rational voter' and rational voting. These notions are generally overblown. They make a great deal of sense, however, with reference to the voter's second shot. Indeed, a voter that knows the returns, that can therefore calculate the winning chances of the runners, surely is a voter engaged in 'rational voting' and/or enabled to perform rationally. The upshot is that while any electoral system intent upon containing party proliferation must in some manner compress the voter's choices, the double ballot softens and somewhat transforms this constraint into intelligent choosing.

It is not only the voter, however, that is allowed a second choice and, by implication, a rational choice. A parallel freedom of second-choosing is equally allowed to the parties and their candidates. For after the first round the parties enter a bargaining game of *rational exchanges* among themselves by signalling to each other that 'my candidate' will pull out from district A if 'your candidate' withdraws, in exchange, from district B. To be sure, these exchange bargains are by no means easy to strike. They are easier between adjacent parties, also because their contiguity suggests that their respective voters are amenable to switching among them. Conversely, exchange bargains between non-contiguous and/or relatively distant parties are not only difficult to strike, but are also more likely to fail in the transfer of their respective electorates. Be that as it may, the important implication of the above is that when parties know that they will be forced into reciprocal exchanges, they will equally be 'rationally forced' into downplaying their ideological differences and thus into playing their competitive game with moderation. The effect of the double ballot system is not only that it brings about (in Duverger's wording) 'flexible' parties, but also that it moderates politics. In the overall, the double ballot punishes ideological politics and rewards pragmatic politics.

My understanding of the 'exchange game' that I have just described is, clearly, a positive one. However, it can also be viewed negatively. In this view the exchange game all too easily spills over into 'improper exchanges', that is, into improper side payments: dispensations of spoils and all sorts of shady political favors. This may often be the case; and yet the argument is, I think, misdirected.

If bad politicians exist, as they do, it does not follow from this that politicians must be made to disappear. If money permits, as it does, usury, the implication cannot be that money should be eliminated. Politics does consist, in no small part, of exchanges and striking deals; and if these deals degenerate into improper payoffs, the conclusion cannot all too simply be that the fault lies in the dealing. Thus, if and when the double ballot degenerates into what Italians call a *mercato delle vacche*, a cow market (whose innuendo is milk mincing),[14] the conclusion need not be that the defect lies in the electoral system. How about the cows? Why are they available? After all these cows exist because the state trespasses into extra-political areas, because it invades the economic sphere (*sub specie* of industrial and managerial state); and conversely cease to exist if the state is made to shrink and is brought back into its natural borders. If we have a spoils problem the correct answer to the problem is: fewer spoils.

Suppose, however, that in a given country spoil sidepayments and pork-barrel politics reach pathological magnitudes. If so, the remedy allowed by the flexibility of the system is to adopt the closed run-off, that is, to admit to the second ballot only the first two runners. Under this arrangement there is no room for bargaining and so the problem is beheaded. On the other hand, the benefits of the bargaining process should not be too lightly surrendered. In the real world something has to give; and if the greater evil is the pork barrel, then let us accept what it costs to dispose of it. But when this is not the case, then the open second ballot is to be preferred to the closed one.

The defenders of the closed run-off argue that with a double ballot system parties can and do bargain anyway, that is, even when the access to the second round is limited to the two top finishers. In this case – so goes the argument – parties can negotiate their reciprocal *do ut des*, their reciprocal exchanges, at the outset. But this is not very plausible. For one, parties that withdraw from the running before trying it admit defeat and engineer, in the longer run, their own disappearance. Secondly, it is very difficult to strike bargains in the dark, that is, before knowing how many votes one actually has (and can give) across the districts in which exchanges make sense. In all likelihood, then, the closed run-off will prompt most parties to try their luck on their own, under the assumptions that a poor showing is better than no showing at all, and that votes wasted on themselves still are votes subtracted from their closest and most disliked competitors.

The difference between open and closed second ballot is – I insist – a veritable and important difference. However, how open or, conversely, how restricted should the access to the run-off be? Here I favor the semi-open or semi-closed solution of allowing access to three-four candidates,[15] on two grounds. Firstly, if the second ballot admits more than four finishers, then it encourages 'blackmail runners' that have no chance of winning but can still make another party lose. At the same time, and secondly, three-to-four final runners are sufficient for allowing the extent of cross-party bargaining that suffices to moderate politics and to deflate artificially blown-up divisiveness.

We are now ready for the question whether the double ballot is also amenable – in spite of its very great variance – to some kind of law-like summation. By and large it is intuitive that in single-member districts the double ballot obtains the same reductive effects of all majoritarian systems, albeit to a lesser and less predictable degree; and that in small multi-member districts the double ballot will perform like a strongly impure proportional system, albeit in a less predictable manner. Why is that? Why the lower predictability? The answer is, obviously enough, that here we have new intervening variables: (i) a second race with reduced runners, (ii) interfered with by cross-party maneuverings and exchanges. And the end result especially depends on (ii), that is to say, on how skillfully (or not) parties manage to strike successful bargains among themselves. This surely is a highly contingent factor, and yet amenable to the rule of thumb that poor bargaining obtains higher reductive effects, while shrewd bargaining allows for the survival of a higher number of parties.[16]

Can we do any better than that? I would say that while the reductive effects on the *number of parties* of the double ballot cannot be generally predicted with any precision, the double ballot does allow a neat prediction of *which parties* (which kind of parties) will be severely underrepresented, often to the point of being squeezed into irrelevance. For the double ballot strongly penalizes the anti-system parties.[17]

So-called anti-system parties are a mixed bag,[18] and may be divided into extremist, extreme and/or isolated parties. Extremist parties are the truly anti-system ones: they advocate (at least in rhetoric) a revolutionary conquest of power, reject and disown 'their' political system, and perform in the activist mode. Extreme parties assume a polity characterized by a wide spectrum of political stances, and are the parties that find themselves located at one of its extreme ends. Thus an extreme party need not be an extremist party. Finally, isolated parties are, purely and simply, non-accepted parties, parties ostracized by the prevailing opinion (especially on value grounds).[19]

Clearly, extremist, extreme and isolated parties shade into each other and are not rejected to a same extent and degree. They all share, however, the handicap of being off limits in terms of vote transfers. With the double ballot system the voters that lose along the way their most preferred candidate transfer their vote, at the run-off, to less preferred but still acceptable candidates. However, this vote changing ends at a no-transfer point beyond which the voter refuses to go. And the extremist-isolated parties stand at the no-transfer pale of voting flexibility. Their fill is the initial one. At the second ballot their votes may go to other parties (to fight greater evils, or punish closest rivals), but they will not receive extra votes. And here they founder.

Can the above be rendered in rule form? Since the double ballot both draws from majoritarian and proportional criteria, the earlier dichotomous distinction between strong and feeble electoral systems needs to be replaced here by a finer slicing between (i) strong, (ii) strong-to-feeble, and (iii) feeble double ballot systems. The double ballot is strong when it requires an absolute majority, and thus with single-member districts and closed access to the run-off. The double ballot is strong-feeble when it requires a high threshold of admission to the run-off (e.g., the current French 12.5 percent); and, inversely, feeble-strong when the threshold of admission is relatively low (e.g., 5–6 percent). Finally, it is feeble when there is no threshold, or when the double ballot performs in multi-member districts. Under this classification, let the rules be:

Rule 1. The strong double ballot will eliminate (from relevancy) the anti-system parties and will severely underrepresent the third 'dispersed' parties that lack sizeable regional and/or district strongholds.

Rule 2. The strong-feeble double ballot will still eliminate the anti-system parties, but allows third dispersed parties to bargain their way into relevance.

Rule 3. The feeble-strong double ballot will underrepresent both the anti-system parties and the minor parties, but may allow them to survive at relevancy levels.

Rule 4. The feeble double ballot obtains the disrepresentative and possibly also the reductive effects of Rule 3 to a lesser and more uncertain extent.[20]

To be sure, the above rules are loose 'tendency rules'. But they do allow for decently precise predictions on a country by country basis, that is, when the context and actual configurations are entered.[21]

Predictions and details aside, the bottom line is how the double ballot relates to governability. I have noted over and over again that no electoral system can ensure, per se, governments empowered to govern – not even the plurality, first-past-the post system. Furthermore, plurality elections are unsuited to highly polarized societies and party systems. Per contra, some form or other of the double ballot can be smoothly applied even to highly polarized settings. And an electoral system that does penalize – as the double ballot surely does – the most-distant, i.e., the most-left and most-rightist (extreme) parties, is doubtlessly a system that eminently facilitates governability under adverse conditions. Which is no small merit.

4.4   WHICH IS BEST?

Majoritarian electoral systems are by now rare; they mostly exist because voters that find them in place get accustomed to them; and have long been under attack in England itself.[22] The attack is sustained – we know – by the reasoning that the uppermost requirement of representative democracy is fair representation, and that representation is fair only when it is proportional. I do not underestimate the power of this reasoning. Still, it is wrong to argue – I believe – that proportional systems are inherently superior to majoritarian systems, and therefore that they are *always* to be preferred. The most influential recent spokesman for this view is Arend Lijphart; and his argument deserves to be looked into at some length.

Lijphart (1968a) started with challenging the notion of Gabriel Almond and others that working democracies were either of the English or Scandinavian type (e.g., Sweden and Norway), and that PR and coalition governments added up to being 'non-working' systems. His counter-example was the Netherlands; and with regard to the Netherlands Lijphart developed the theory of 'consociational democracy' (1968b), which he then extended to Switzerland, Austria and, adventurously enough, Lebanon. Lijphart was absolutely right in holding that a democracy could work even under adverse conditions (especially a fragmented political culture) by having recourse to non-majoritarian, consociational practices; and his consociational democracy construct was a perceptive and important addition to our understanding of democratic governance. Thereafter, however, Lijphart has blown up these premises into a 'grand theory' of a superior form of democracy: consensus democracy. And while I do follow the initial Lijphart, I cannot follow him that far.

The gradual passage from a specific to a general, grand theory is mostly terminological. Consociational democracy is rebaptized 'consensus democracy'; and while the consociational construct presupposed a segmented social structure, the new name for this hinterland is 'plural societies'. Furthermore, the initial construction was typological: consociational democracy was a 'type'. Consensus democracy is displayed, instead, as a 'model'. Types we know how to handle (logically and methodologically). Models we do not even know what they are, but are assumed to be entities of a much more majestic status.

Now, to change a word is not simply to change a word: it changes a meaning. Words have a semantic projection, that is to say, they convey interpretations.[23] Thus, if we say 'consensus democracy' we already have in our hand of cards the winning trump. Can anybody ever hold that a non-consented democracy is as good as a consented one? Likewise, if we say 'plural societies' – indeed a very bland and diluted labeling – the suggestion that inevitably creeps into our minds is that since all societies are, in some manner and to some extent, plural, then Lijphart's recipe is indeed good for all societies.

To be sure, between the first and the last Lijphart the changes are not only of wordings. The *necessary condition* for the successful working of a consociational democracy is an 'elite cooperation' that intentfully counters the disintegrative tendencies of their societies; but this necessary and most crucial condition disappears in the definition of consensus democracy. Likewise, the defining characteristic of the segmented societies that Lijphart had originally in mind was that their structure of cleavages was not crosscutting but instead cumulative and self-reinforcing. Read now how Lijphart defines his plural societies: 'societies that are sharply divided along religious, ideological, linguistic, cultural, ethnic or racial lines into virtually separate subsocieties' (1984a, p. 22). The two noteworthy points of this definition are, first, that it is far too strong for 'plural' (here the word plural appears a misnomer); and, second, that the 'cumulative cleavage' underpinning is fudged. Each reader is thus left to decide on his own how much 'sharpness' makes for a sharply divided society, and how much 'separateness' makes for virtually separate subsocieties. In the end, it is the word plural (not its definition) that carries the day on the force of its own semantic wishy-washiness.

Pulling the nets to shore, what is consensus democracy? In Lijphart's own summary (1984a, pp. 23, 30):

> The consensus model of democracy may be described in terms of eight elements which stand in sharp contrast to the majoritarian characteristics of the Westminster model . . . All of the eight elements aim at restraining majority rule by requiring or encouraging: the *sharing of power* between the majority and the minority (grand coalitions), the *dispersal of power* (among executive and legislature, two legislative chambers, and several minority parties), *a fair distribution of power* (proportional representation), . . . and a *formal limit on power* (by means of the minority veto).[24]

The above is indeed a roundabout power-massacre. Nice? Perhaps not, for the merits of each of the above elements can be found to have equivalent or even greater demerits. (i) Grand coalitions obscure responsibility to the utmost and are, as a rule, more heterogeneous and therefore more easily gridlocked than minimum-winning coalitions. (ii) Dispersal of power among executive and legislature easily becomes a messy and wasteful confusion of power; and a dispersal of power across several minority parties adds profusion to confusion. (iii) Proportional representation is, per se, fine; but hardly so in the extreme form recommended by Lijphart, which includes *proporz*, quota-type allocations and duplications across the civil service and in public funding. (iv) Finally, to admit the minority veto as a major and normal means of limiting power is to admit a shuddering principle. But above all it is the contrast between a majoritarian and a consensus model that is both biased and overworked.

The contrast is biased because its wording conveys, wittingly or not, that majoritarianism is conflict maximizing or, at any rate, poor at conflict handling. I would say, instead, that consensus management is the very essence of any and all democratic governance, and that there is no a priori reason for holding that the Westminster method cannot handle the consensus-conflict maze as well as, or even better than, the consensus-consociational method. Indeed, Lijphart's argument can be turned around all the way. By facilitating something you make it happen. The more you given in, the more you are asked to give. And what is not discouraged becomes in fact encouraged. If you reward divisions and divisiveness (and this is precisely what *proporz* and veto power do), you increase and eventually heighten divisions and divisiveness. In the end, then, Lijphart's machinery may well engender more consensus-breaking than consensus-making. For peace at all costs is the worst possible way of averting wars. Furthermore, and in the second place, Lijphart's contrast is overworked because in any and all democracy the majority principle is, and has to be, affirmed as follows: that the will of the majority is entitled to prevail within the limits of the respect of minority rights. So, majoritarianism is always limited or restrained. If otherwise, it is democracy itself that self-destructs (Sartori, 1987, pp. 31–34 and 132–33).

In the winding up, Lijphart smoothly and almost imperceptibly leads us from the thesis that consociational democracy is best for segmented, heterogeneous and/or polarized societies, to the utterly different thesis that it is a superior 'consensus model' for virtually all societies. But no. Consociational democracy is a cross-pressured system held together by countervailing, solidaristic elites bent upon neutralizing the centrifugal pulls of their societies; consensus democracy is, instead, a one-way slope that leads to a self-reinforcing system of minority appetites. Thus I subscribe to the first formula, but cannot subscribe to the second one.[25]

To be sure, the case for PR does not need, as with Lijphart, a nesting in any grand theory. The case for PR can be encapsulated in the simple and straightforward argument that it is representative government, not good government, that is of essence, and the very essence, of democratic politics. Is this a sure winner, a crushing argument? I think not because its propounders seemingly ignore that representative government is a shorthand for *representative and responsible* government, and that the two qualifications go hand in hand. And a further point is this: that responsible government has two sides, two faces. On the one hand responsible implies 'responsiveness'; but on the other hand it implies independent responsibility, the kind of behavior that consists of 'acting responsibly', with all the competence, prudence and ability that any representative is required to muster *vis-à-vis* those represented.[26] The complete and correct argument thus is that democracy demands good (responsible) government as much as it demands responsive government, and that the two elements cannot be disjoined.

So, what is best? In my previous assessments I have given the pro's and the con's of each electoral system. Majoritarian-plurality systems are best, or at any rate at their best, when they manufacture a two-party system which produces, in turn, single-party 'responsible' government. But this does not easily happen. Thus plurality elections are more appropriately defended on the grounds of what I have called a diluted governability claim (*supra* 4.1), that is, by arguing that they keep party fragmentation low, and are therefore more likely to be conducive to effective government than PR systems. On the other hand, and at the other extreme, it should be recognized that a single-member district system may also be conducive to the dismemberment of a polity into sheer local and localistic politics.

As regards PR, I have recognized its great historical merits and have acknowledged that in its impure forms it generally obtains a satisfactory blending of adequate representation and sufficient governability. PR is best, then, when corrected. I equally concede that PR may be helpful and indeed necessary for particularly difficult societies – as in the arguments of

Nordlinger (1972) and of the first Lijphart. On the other hand, in its pure form PR generally backfires; and in the 'extremist package' recommended by Lijphart its defects boomerang and PR may turn out to be a kiss of death.

Reformers have now begun to play with the idea that what is best is a mixture, a blending, of plurality and PR. This idea draws from a misperception of the German system, which is mixed in terms of voting criteria but not in terms of outcome, which is fully proportional for the entire *Bundestag* (*supra* 2.2). Since a mixed system is supposed, instead, to produce a body whose composition combines a proportional with a non-proportional representation of its members, and thus a semi-proportional and/or semi-majoritarian outcome, the German case does not speak to this intent. A truly mixed system is, then, a system whose parliamentary membership reflects a proportion countered by a disproportion. Thus the salient, current instances of truly mixed parliaments are illustrated by the Italian, Japanese and Russian cases. More precisely, Italy has adopted in August 1993 a mix of 75 percent plurality and 25 percent PR; a few months later Japan has abandoned its old electoral system for a 50/50 mix of plurality and PR (indeed pure PR);[27] and in December 1993 Russia has been swiftly called to vote for its new lower House (called State Duma) under the same half-and-half combination.[28]

Regardless of ratios, I believe these plurality-PR couplings to be a mismarriage, a very unsound and counterproductive arrangement. In Russia's case any electoral system would have produced erratic results; but certainly Russians have been ill-advised in starting from scratch with a schizoid electoral system that either encourages shots in the dark (with plurality) or splintering (with PR), and that is of no help whatsoever in shaping the future. In the Italian case the electoral test has still to occur, but my prophecy is that its 75 percent plurality part will not engineer (given the Italian distributions) any cohesive bipolar realignment, while its proportional part will maintain the fragmentation at dama-ging levels. In the Japanese case I cannot tell (if the reform stands as it is) which weird distortions will result from the plurality constituencies, but the PR nationwide constituency will certainly allow a fragmentation that will be soon regretted.

To be sure, there is a difference between switching to a plurality-PR mixture from a formerly majoritarian or from a formerly proportional system. In the first case a country loses single-party government but will not develop, at least in the short run, excessive party fragmentation (for the habit of two-party voting will not be lost overnight). In this case, then, the switch can be interpreted as a soft landing to a corrected and blunted plurality. In the second case, instead, a passing from PR to a partial plurality simply is a wrong move. But in any case the principle is – I submit – that electoral systems should have *one* logic which conforms to their purpose. In Farquharson's (1969) terminology, PR calls for 'sincere voting', i.e., permits the voter to freely express his or her first preference, whereas majoritarian elections require 'strategic voting', i.e., voters that concentrate their ballots on the likely winners (and are thus required to express second best and 'calculated' preferences). So voters cannot and should not be asked to make, all in one, majoritarian (strategic) and proportional (sincere) kinds of choices – for this is a sure manner to confuse their behavior, as well as a probable way of obtaining parliaments that cannot serve any purpose. Perhaps the advocates of plurality–PR hybrids believe that they are bringing together the best of two worlds; but they are likely to obtain, instead, a bastard-producing hybrid which combines their defects.

Understandably, in any country any return from the openness of PR to the strictures of majoritarianism traumatizes the vested interests and habits. But if this switch is made, then the good way of making it is via an open double ballot system.[29] And this is a further reason for calling the attention of scholars to a formula that most experts seemingly ignore or patently misunderstand. Do I conclude, then, that if there is a 'best' electoral system, this is the double ballot system in its wide range of adaptability, of possible formulations? Yes, that would be my general preference; under the proviso, to be sure, that no electoral system is best for all seasons.

NOTES

1. Sartori, 1968a, p. 469. (Reference to a French-type is, of course, historical.) I quote myself in an old writing because I have been charged of missing that 'electoral systems should be classified and evaluated according to the principles of representation' (Nohlen, 1984a, pp. 84–87). This is not so, and in fact I agree, throughout many writings, with Nohlen's point.

2. For instance, in England in 1974 Labor won the government with 37.2 percent of the vote against 39.9 percent of the Conservatives. Still worse, in New Zealand in 1978 and 1981 it was the party that came second in the vote that obtained an absolute majority of seats.

3. E.g. Richard Rose (1983, pp. 40–41) indicates that 'the difference in proportionality between the median election under proportional representation and plurality systems is very limited: 7%;' and his evidence (in Table 8) indicates, furthermore, that some plurality countries display greater proportionality than some PR countries. The argument is repeated in Rose 1984 (pp. 74–75 and Table 7.1) where the difference in proportionality becomes 8%. But Rose misses the point that I am about to make.

4. As attested by the English liberals. E.g., in the British elections of 1983 the Alliance (their label at the time) obtained 25.4% of the vote and only 3.5% of the seats. In this instance the cost of a Labour seat in the Commons was 40,000 votes, the cost of an Alliance seat 400,000 votes (ten times as much).

5. Prior to these conditions it must be recalled that the entire argument hinges on having rules that separate irrelevant from relevant parties. To illustrate, Rose asserts that 'There is no tendency for non-PR electoral systems to produce a two-party Parliament. In the six [plurality] countries reviewed here there are an average of five parties in each Parliament, and as many as nine parties in the British parliament' (Rose, 1984, p. 78). But this is playing with statistics that play with meaningless numbers.

6. Unless they happen to perform as predominant party systems with single-party government (Sartori, 1976, pp. 192–201). This has been the case, e.g., of Japan between 1954–1993, of Norway and Sweden between the Thirties and the Eighties, and of Spain as of 1982.

7. The Polish 1991 parliamentary election had 29 political groups winning seats in the Seym, with 8 parties in the percentage range between 16.9 and 6.0, and thus in the range of relevance. The introduction in the 1993 September election of a 5 percent threshold has helped reduce this fragmentation to six parties, which are still too many and too distant (ideologically) among themselves to allow for working (homogeneous) coalition governments.

8. The caveat is, again, that this applies to parliamentary systems. Presidential systems require a different analysis (*infra* ch. 5).

9. Bear in mind, however, that my argument is structural and therefore that when I assert that homogeneous coalitions do or can do better than heterogeneous ones I am simply pointing to a favorable condition. To say *nihil obstat*, nothing prevents, is just to say that. Even homogeneous coalitions may thus turn out to be highly litigious.

10. The nineteenth century parties of notables and/or of opinion were 'internally created' in the sense that they first were born in the parliamentary arena (as alliances and fusions among MP's), and then expanded outward as electoral, vote-seeking parties. Instead, socialist, Catholic and similar movements were born outside of, and in opposition-negation to, the existing order, and have thus been aptly called by Duverger 'externally created'.

11. See, more extensively, Fisichella, 1982, pp. 254–55, 263–66, 274–85.

12. It is fair to recall that Duverger has subsequently been – in the face of the experience of the Fifth Republic – a staunch defender of the double ballot, whose adoption he strongly recommended (if to no avail) for the Italian electoral reform of 1993.

13. Reference is made (see *supra* 2.1) to whether pre-electoral primaries should be open or closed, to the distortion brought about by a participation limited to 'intense' publics, and to the ease with which primaries can be manipulated and have become media over-exposed. A primary-like selection that is part and parcel of the electoral process is – vis-á-vis these problems – a problem-free solution.

14. The American translation of the Italian expression would be 'horse trading'. However, a *mercato delle vacche* points to a far greater order of magnitude both of the payoffs and of their impropriety.

15. There are two ways of obtaining this level of openness. The straightforward one is to stipulate that the run-off admits the first three or four first-run candidates. Alternatively one can have recourse to thresholds of admission tailored to the foreseeable voting distributions.

16. This explains, I believe, why Fisichella (1982, p. 267) maintains that the double ballot may not reduce the number of parties. This outcome assumes, however, a rare, near-perfect bargaining.

17. This applies, we are told, only if the anti-system party does not happen to be the relative majority party. Yes and no, however, The closed double ballot would wipe out even a 40 percent party if dangerous enough, in the perception of the remaining voters, to unite them all in voting against its candidate.

18. I deal with the concept and definition of 'anti-system' in Sartori, 1976, pp. 132–34.

19. E.g., the Italian neo-fascist party, the MSI, which by all standards has been a 'normal' party, and yet has always been kept, up until 1993, out of government. Currently, xenophobic parties that oppose immigrants (e.g., Le Pen's National Front in France) are equally isolated parties. The same might apply to a strongly religious party in a laical context, or to a Christian party in an Islamic area. The reasons for exclusion and segregation can be many.

20. I propose a somewhat different set of rules in Sartori, 1984, pp. 39–40. I understand these earlier rules as complementary to the ones formulated here.

21. Take, for example, the extreme case of the French 1993 elections in which a 39 percent of the vote has given to the center-right alliance 80 percent of the seats in the national assembly. Under the existing formal arrangements France falls under my Rule 2; but since relevant third parties have by now ceased to exist, they cannot bargain their way in. Hence the rule that actually applies is that part of Rule 1 which predicts the elimination or downsizing into irrelevance of the anti-system parties (and, indeed, Le Pen's 'isolated' party obtained no seats with 12 percent of the vote). As for the truly enormous discrepancy between votes and seats, this abnormal disrepresentation is 'normal' in any plurality system with an interval of almost 20 percentage points – as was the case in France – between the winners and the socialist losers. For instance, in New Zealand in 1990 a swing of less than 10 percent of the vote

gave the conservatives (the National party) 68 out of the 97 seats in its single-chamber parliament; and in the October 1993 Canadian election the ruling Conservative party was wiped out, plummeting from 157 to 2 seats.

22. And more than that in New Zealand, where a referendum of September 1992 supported a switch to a mixed plurality-PR system (on a half-and-half basis). The English debate in favor of PR is well represented by the classic work of Lakeman and Lambert (1955). More recent criticisms of the plurality system are in S. E. Finer ed. (1979).

23. This is a constant theme of all my work. See especially Sartori 1979, *passim*; and Sartori 1984b, pp. 15–22.

24. For a more concise characterization see Lijphart, 1977, p. 24, where the elements are reduced to four. The 1977 book already adopts 'plural' but still holds to 'consociational'.

25. A broader assessment of the consociational democracy theme is in Sartori, 1987, pp. 238–40, where my conclusion reads that 'along a continuum whose polar ends are "always majoritarianism" and "never majoritarianism", the concrete democracies are likely to be all the more majoritarian the more they are consensual, homogeneous (culturally), and non-segmented (in their structure of cleavages), and all the less majoritarian (i.e., consociational) the less these characteristics obtain'.

26. See Sartori 1968a. This connotation comes neatly to the fore when we speak of 'irresponsible government', an expression that is well understood to mean incompetent, silly, demagogic and/or budget-busting government.

27. At the close of this writing, however, the new formula had only been approved by the Lower House, not by the Upper one.

28. Remember that also New Zealand is likely to switch, in 1995, from the first-past-the-post to a mixed plurality–PR system. In 1993 Venezuela too has switched to a German-like formula. But here I am concerned with the impact of electoral mixes upon parliamentary government, not presidential government.

29. Within this formula the landing can be softened further – for instance by removing all admission thresholds to the second round and allowing for a modicum (say, 15 percent) of proportional redistribution in national party lists for the parties that abandon the running after the first round. In this manner the minor parties can be saved from outright decapitation without interfering with the double ballot logic of electoral behavior.

Part Two
Presidentialism and Parliamentarism

5 Presidentialism

5.1 DEFINING 'PRESIDENTIAL SYSTEM'

Just as electoral systems are divided into majoritarian and proportional, so are democratic political systems generally divided into presidential and parliamentary. However, the latter distinction is more difficult to draw than the former one. Sure, presidential and parliamentary systems can be defined by mutual exclusion. Sure, a presidential system is non-parliamentary and, conversely, a parliamentary system is non-presidential. But the distribution of the real world cases into these two classes obtains impermissible bedfellows. The reason for this is, on the one hand, that presidential systems are for the most part inadequately defined; and, on the other hand, that parliamentary systems differ so widely among themselves as to render their common name a misnomer for a deceitful togetherness. We shall look into this later. Here, and first, we are required to define presidential systems and thereby to make sure that they are not confused with facade presidential forms or erroneously perceived as mixes, as quasi- or near-parliamentary presidentialisms.

The first defining criterion for a presidential system is the direct or direct-like popular election of the head of state for a fixed time span (that may range from four to eight years). This criterion is doubtlessly a necessary defining condition; but by no means a sufficient one. Austria, Iceland and Ireland have recourse to a direct popular election of their presidents and yet are only, at most, facade presidentialisms. Regardless of what the constitution says about their power prerogatives,[1] the presidents in question are little more than figureheads, and Austria, Iceland and Ireland perform in all respects like parliamentary systems. These countries cannot be classified, then, among the presidential ones, in spite of their popularly elected presidents.[2]

A second defining criterion is that in presidential systems the government, or the executive, is neither appointed nor dismissable via a parliamentary vote. Governments are a presidential prerogative: it is the president that discretionally appoints and discharges cabinet members. To be sure, a president may pick his ministers in a manner that pleases his parliament; even so, cabinet members are and remain presidential appointees. Let it be immediately noted that the criterion in question is not violated if a parliament is given the power of censuring individual cabinet ministers, or even by the rare cases in which a parliamentary censure entails that a minister must be removed from office.[3] The criterion is not violated because in either case it is still the president that unilaterally retains the nominating power and fills cabinet posts as he or she sees fit.

Do criterion one plus criterion two suffice to identify a presidential system? I would say almost, but not quite. For it must be very clear that a pure presidential system does not allow for any kind of 'dual authority' between the president and his cabinet. On this score Lijphart proposes the criterion 'a one person executive'. But this is perhaps a too narrow pinpointing: it implies that the head of state *must* also be the head of government. True, this is generally the case. Still, I prefer a somewhat looser formulation, such as this: that the line of authority is neatly streamlined from the president down. In short, the third criterion is that the president directs the executive.

So, a political system is presidential if, and only if, the head of state (president) i) results from popular election, ii) during his or her pre-established tenure cannot be discharged by a parliamentary vote, and iii) heads or otherwise directs the governments that he or she appoints. When these three conditions are jointly met, then we doubtlessly have a pure presidential system – or so says my definition.[4]

We still have a loose end to tie up. The first criterion reads, in full, that a president must result from a direct or 'direct-like' election. How open-ended is that? Direct-like accounts for the United States and for countries such as Argentina and, formerly, Chile (up until Allende), whose President is elected by parliament when no candidate receives an absolute majority of the popular vote. Since the established practice in such cases is to elect the candidate that has obtained the popular relative majority, this kind of indirect election can be assimilated to a direct one. Bolivia practices instead a parliamentary choosing among the three front runners (both in 1985 and 1989 it picked the second one) and therefore represents a dubious direct-like case. On the other hand, until 1988 Finland was definitely not direct-like: the elected presidential electoral college was the true president-maker in that its freedom of choice was unrestricted. The cut-off point is, then, whether the intermediary body (electoral college or parliament) is allowed choices of its own. If it performs as a rubber stamp, then the difference between direct and indirect popular election is immaterial; if it can make choices, then criterion one is somewhat violated (but see *infra* 7.3).

The general point is this: that presidential systems (just like parliamentary systems) are such, and hang together, on account of a *systemic logic* of their own. Thus, before reassigning presidentialism to another class – whether semi-presidentialism, near-parliamentarism, and the like – we must check whether a given variance violates that logic or not. What if a president is entitled to dissolve parliament? What if parliament is entitled to impose the dismissal of cabinet members? What if a president can be recalled by a popular vote? Do these and other anomalies bring about a different mechanism that abides by a different logic? If the answer is yes, then let us see what kind of new mechanism we have, and let us reclassify a presidential system accordingly. But let us not rush headlong into discovering or inventing 'new systems' every time that a country borrows a device from another system.

Under this proviso I trust that we now have a definition that neatly sorts out what 'presidentialism' includes and, conversely, excludes. On its basis we come up, today, with some 20 countries, mostly concentrated in Latin America.[5] The reason that Europe has no pure presidential systems, whilst we find them from Canada down through all of the two Americas, is historical and does not attest to any deliberate choice. When the European states started practicing constitutional government, all (except France, that became a republic in 1870) were monarchies; and monarchies already have a hereditary head of state. But while in Europe there was no room (at least until 1919) for elected presidents, in the New World almost all the new states became independent as republics (Brazil and, in a manner, Mexico, being the temporary exceptions), and therefore had to have elected heads of state, i.e., presidents. The division between presidential versus parliamentary systems did not result, then, from any theory that debated whether one form was superior to the other. But the time has come for this debate to occur and, thus, for a comparative assessment of how the two systems perform.

By and large, presidentialism has performed poorly. With the sole exception of the United States, all other presidential systems have been fragile – they have regularly succumbed to coups and breakdowns.[6] However, the exception of the United States, lonely as it is, is an important one. Furthermore, the United States provides the original from which all the other presidential systems are derived. So from here we start.

5.2   THE AMERICAN PROTOTYPE

The Washington model is characterized, more than by any other single feature, by the division-separation of power between President and Congress. This separation is not easily spelled out. For Neustadt (1960, p. 33) the Founding Fathers did not create a government of 'separated powers' but, instead, 'a government of separated institutions *sharing* power'. But Jones (1990, p. 3) corrects: we now 'have a government of separated institutions *competing for* shared power'; and he ultimately perceives the American polity as a 'truncated system'. These and other important nuances notwithstanding, the essence of the matter is this: separation consists of 'separating' the executive from parliamentary support, whereas power sharing means that the executive stands on, and falls without, the support of parliament.[7] And on this criterion what the United States has is indeed power separation.

With power division, then, a parliament cannot interfere in the internal affairs, in the *interna corporis*, of the executive realm, and especially cannot dismiss (impeachment aside) a president. By virtue of the same logic, or of the same principle, power separation implies that a president cannot dissolve a parliament. And this is indeed the case in the United States and in most presidential systems. But what if a president is given such power? Does this constitute a violation of the separation principle? Yes, even though my inclination is to consider the power of dissolution of parliament an anomaly that does not transform – if all my three defining criteria apply – a presidential system into another kind of system. True, the power of dissolving parliament reinforces the presidential power; but the efficacy of this deterrent is generally over-estimated and, in any event, on this ground alone I do not see sufficient grounds for reclassifying a presidential structure.

The American system is also characterized by most authors as a system of checks and balances. Right; but this is hardly a distinctive qualification, for all veritable constitutional systems are systems of checks and balances. The point is that we can have checks and balances without power separation, and that the uniqueness of American-type presidentialism precisely is that it checks and balances power by dividing it. Therefore (I insist) *the* defining and central feature of the Washington model is an executive power that subsists in separateness – on its own right as an autonomous body.

This does not imply in the least that the American president is indifferent as to whether he may, or may not, enjoy Congressional support. Indeed, the more we have a divided power structure, the more we need – it would seem – a 'united government', i.e., a same majority in control of the executive and of Congress. This has been for a century and a half both the theory and the practice of American governance. However, the prevailing pattern has now become one of 'divided government'. Eisenhower was, in 1954 and then in 1957, the first President after seventy-two years to be confronted by a Congress controlled by the opposition party. Since then 'from 1955 through 1992 the government was divided for twenty-six of thirty-eight years'; and 'from 1969 through 1992 divided government prevailed in twenty of twenty-four years' (Sund-quist, 1992, p. 93). True, the Clinton presidency has re-established in 1993 an undivided majority. Yet the trend has unequivocally been, in the last forty years, a trend of minority presidents, of presidents whose party did not hold a majority in the Houses. While Republicans have held the White House for all but four years (with Carter) between 1968 and 1992, Democrats have constantly controlled one House and (but for six years) both Houses since 1955.

To most observers this appears to be a momentous turn-around which confronts the American system with deadlock and gridlock. However, according to David Mayhew there is no reason to worry, for in his findings 'unified as opposed to divided control has not made an important difference in . . . the enactment of a standard kind of important legislation: . . . important laws have materialized at a rate largely unrelated to party control' (1991, p. 4). But Mayhew is, I believe, quite wrong. The difference between unified and divided govern-ment cannot be belittled, and the reason why this difference does not show up in his findings makes the case for the American system more worrisome than ever.[8] I come back to this shortly. I first wish to state the full case as I see it.

The basic assumption about presidential systems is that they are conducive to strong and effective government – both *per se* and in comparison to parliamentary systems. But this is an assumption that stands on thin ice. The fact that the American system has long coped with its problems does not detract from the fact that a divided power structure engineers paralysis and stalemates better than any other. And, indeed, does the American system still work? Looking back, we see that the division of power has been compensated not only by consonant majorities, by the coinciding of the president's majority with the parliamentary one, but also, in custom, by consociational practices, especially bi-partisan concurrence in foreign politics.

However – and barring an unlikely return to enduring cycles of undivided government – the pattern that has emerged from the Fifties onward confronts us with a split, antagonis-tically divided polity whose two major component elements perceive their respective electoral interest to be, across the board, in the failure of the other institution. For a Democratic controlled Congress to go along with a Republican President is to help another Republican presidency. Conversely, a minority president (in Congress) seeking to restore undivided government is prompted to run against Congress playing, as it were, the blame game.

Ironically, then, the belief that presidential systems are strong systems draws on the worst possible structural arrangement – a divided power defenseless against divided government – and fails to realize that the American system works, or has worked, *in spite of* its constitution – hardly *thanks to* its constitution. To the extent to which it is still able to perform, it requires, in order to unblock itself, three factors: ideological unprincipledness, weak and undisciplined parties, and locality centered politics. On these counts a president can win over the congressional votes that he may need by 'horse trading' constituency favors. We thus end up with the institutionalization of pork-barrel politics – nothing much to be admired. And what we have, structurally, is in fact a weak state.

We may now revert to Mayhew's findings that the divided party control of the presidency and of Congress does not appear to affect and worsen in any significant way the legislative output of Congress. Let us assume, for the sake of the argument, that this finding does hit upon something. If so, however, it does not speak to the point intended by Mayhew but, rather, to the increasing atomization of the American party. That is to say that the factor or variable at play is the crossing of party lines in Congressional voting. Whether a president has, or does not have, 'his majority' in Congress matters and makes a difference on the assumption that the notion of majority is a meaningful one, that there is something there that hangs together and acts cohesively. If, however, a majority exists only on paper, if it has to be assembled occasion by occasion, then it stands to reason that the difference between united and divided government may make little difference. The point thus becomes that even when the majority is undivided on paper, the reality of the matter is that today an American president never has a true and reliable majority in Congress.

To be sure, the interest of a Democratic congress is to have a Democratic president that succeeds. It is also evident that there must be, for the consumption of public opinion, some showing that united government does provide 'unity' of support, that is, greater support than otherwise. Yet the overriding consideration has become, for each member of Congress, how well his or her voting record fares, vote by vote, in their districts. It is widely admitted that American parties are little more than *electoral parties*, and such only in the feeble sense that they provide labels for two candidates to run their campaigns one against the other in single-member districts. But are they any more than that as *parliamentary parties*? I would say that the increasing dissolution of the electoral party must somehow reflect itself also at the Congressional level.[9] We are thus witnessing an increased and increasing localistic, constituency driven fragmentation of the American congressional-legislative party (though a lesser one, for obvious reasons, in the Senate). And a parliament in which politics becomes retail politics (*supra* 4.1), in which more and more members perform as constituency lobbyists, as constituency errand boys, is a parliament in which majorities easily become a fleeting, vaporous entity. Let us hear on that from an astute observer, from Nelson Polsby (1993, p. 33), who writes:

> In the practical politics of today, legislation frequently requires a complicated sort of agreement: a coalition must be built that crosses . . . party. This coalition is the product of a series of negotiations not only on the substance of various measures but also on the apportionment of credit for the benefits those measures may generate and blame for the pain they may cause . . . Passing legislation that causes pain is thus a risky thing for elected officials to do . . . Amazingly, sometimes they do it, if a deal can be worked out to share the blame.

Polsby knows his characters and portrays them well. But can the process that he describes be called coalition building? I realize that 'coalition' is used sloppily, in the American politics field, as a blanket term for almost everything. Still, coalition is here a misleading term. Coalitions, proper, did exist in

Congress in the past, for the Southern Democrats did perform as a coalition-like bloc. Perhaps coalitions, proper, still exist today. But what Polsby describes is definitely not a coalitional state of affairs. Coalitions *are* agreements: but not single-issue, day by day agreements. The notion of coalition assumes – in order to be meaningful – a modicum of solidity, that is to say, some kind of enduring understanding across a congruent range of issues. Overnight coalitions are not coalitions; and the deals described by Polsby are not coalition-like; they are much more patchwork-like. The point is thus rejoined that with daily, piecemeal collages we do not obtain real majorities. One of the major stakes of the 'reunited government' of President Clinton's administration surely is the economic and deficit-reducing package submitted to Congress in August 1993; a package that was approved (after much wheeling and dealing) with a two-vote majority in the House, and a bare one-vote margin (the vote of the vice-president that presides) in the Senate. Does that attest to a majority supported president? Hardly, I would say.

The bottom line still is, as V.O. Key put it, that 'common partisan control of executive and legislatures does not assure energetic government, but division of party control precludes it' (1965, p. 688). However, another line has to be added to the bottom one, namely, that common partisan control by no means assures a common partisan majority. Regardless, then, of whether the American government happens to be divided or undivided, in either case much of its decision-making requires issue-by-issue localistic side-payments leading to ill-made mosaics rather than to sound compromises. The American system works (in its manner) because Americans are determined to make it work. It is as simple as that and, by the same token, that difficult. For Americans do have a constitutional machine made for gridlock; a defect that shows in all its might when their presidentialism is exported.

5.3 THE LATIN AMERICAN EXPERIENCE

As we leave the United States we naturally land in Latin America. It is here that the bulk of presidential systems reside.

And it is equally here that presidential systems display a worrisome record of fragility and instability.

In terms of longevity, to date Costa Rica is the best performer, for it has remained 'unbroken' since 1949, followed by Venezuela, continuous since 1958, Colombia (since 1974), and Peru (which returned to civilian government in 1979).[10] Most Latin American countries (notably Argentina, Uruguay, Brazil, Chile) have reestablished their presidential democracy only in the 1980s.[11] And while the last South American bastion of old-style dictatorship – Paraguay – has fallen in 1989, a considerable number of countries in the area still qualify as uncertain democracies and/or as polities 'highly vulnerable to breakdown overthrow' (Diamond et al. 1989, p. xviii): for example, Ecuador, Bolivia, Honduras, Guatemala and the Dominican Republic;[12] let alone Nicaragua, which reverted in 1990 to democracy under Sandinista guardianship. In other areas, the Philippines is again, since 1986, presidentially democratic but has yet to prove whether and how it can perform.[13] All in all, then, the record of the presidentially governed countries range – but for one exception – from poor to dismal and prompts us to wonder whether their political problem might not be presidentialism itself.

It is always speculative to separate politics from its economic, social and cultural substratum. And in the case of Latin America it must be especially acknowledged that the difficulties of presidential government relate to, and are mightily intensified by, economic stagnation, glaring inequalities, and socio-cultural legacies. Yet the one handle that we have for confronting and solving problems is politics. Granted that politics can make and often does make matters worse, still it is from 'good politics' that we expect the good things that we seek.

What is wrong, then, with Latin American presidentialisms? The previous analysis of the model, of the U.S. prototype, facilitates the answer. That the presidential systems are strong systems of energetic government has never been quite true for the U.S., and is clearly an illusion leading to delusion in the countries that seek inspiration from the Washington model. One problem is, of course, that many Latin American presidentialisms stand upon 'wrong' party systems.[14] But the major line of argument, and the one to be pursued first, is that Latin American presidents are by no means as all-powerful as they may appear. Quite to the contrary, 'most Latin American Presidents have had trouble accomplishing their agendas. They have held most of the power for initiating policy but have found it hard to get support for implementing policy' (Mainwaring, 1990, p. 162).

But if this is so, why not seek remedy in reinforcing the power of presidents? This path has in fact been pursued, for most Latin American presidents do have more extensive powers than an American president. In many cases they are given the line-item veto on bills that is being repeatedly denied to the White House; they are largely permitted, albeit to different extents, to govern by decree; and they are often allowed extensive emergency powers.[15] And steps are still taken in order to reinforce presidential power.[16] However, the prevalent current mood is, rather, to clip the president's wings,[17] for the past, repeated dictatorial seizures of power are perceived – at times rightly, though often wrongly – to result from their all-powerfulness. Be that as it may, the problem ultimately resides in the separation of power principle; a separation that keeps the Latin American presidentialisms in perennial, unsteady oscillation between power abuse and power deficiency.

We seemingly have, here, a Gordian knot; a knot for which Juan Linz and, in his wake, a number of important scholars see no solution other than the proverbial one of cutting it. Linz and others have thus reached the conclusion that the remedy is not – in Latin America – in improving presidentialism, but in dismissing it altogether and in adopting in its stead a parliamentary form of government. The Linzian argument was formulated in 1985, and its gist was, and remains, that presidentialism is less likely than parliamentarism to sustain stable democratic regimes (see Linz, 1990, 1994). His central point is not, however, that a presidential structure is conducive to structural stalemate but, rather and more generally, that presidential systems are 'rigid' while parliamentary systems are 'flexible', and that flexibility is to be preferred to rigidity especially because flexibility is risk-minimizing. Thus the Linzian case essentially rests on the point that a flexible, parliamentary type of polity is far less risk exposed – on account of its self-correcting mechanisms – than a rigid one. As Valenzuela felicitously encapsulates it, 'The crises of parliamentary systems are crises of government, not regime' (1987, p. 34). No doubt, the point is well taken. No doubt, presidential systems cannot handle major crises.[18] Nonetheless it seems to me that the argument cannot be left at that. In the first place, one of the possible alternatives of presidentialism is semi-presidentialism; and I shall argue that semi-presidentialism largely takes care of the rigidity problem, that it affords the flexibility that presidentialism lacks (*infra*, ch. 7). In the second place, and above all, the Linzian proposal fails to convincingly explain why and how a switch to parliamentarism would solve the governability problems that presidentialism either generates or leaves unresolved.[19]

5.4 IS PARLIAMENTARISM A REMEDY?

Whether parliamentary systems are superior to presidential ones is an issue that must await the analysis of parliamentarism (*infra* ch. 6). At the moment I can only address the transition from the American-like to a European-like system on the basis of this simple admonishment: that parliamentary democracy cannot perform – in any of its many varieties – unless it is served by *parliamentary fit* parties, that is to say, parties that have been socialized (by failure, duration, and appropriate incentives) into being relatively cohesive and/or disciplined bodies. Mind you, the above is not always true for presidential systems, for which the argument is – we know – that under conditions of divided government stalemate is avoided precisely by party indiscipline. Instead, and indeed, disciplined parties are a *necessary condition* for the 'working' of parliamentary systems. Conversely put, with undisciplined parties parliamentary systems become non-working assembly systems.

   The question thus is: if Latin American countries adopted a parliamentary system, would their parliamentary performance be any better than the assemblear one of much of continental Europc all the way up to the twenties and thirties? I very much doubt it, for it is clearly the case that the bulk of Latin America does not have, and is still far from acquiring, parliamentary fit parties. Brazil eminently speaks to the point; and since Brazil did go as far as to submit to a referendum, in 1993, the choosing of parliamentarism, let me pause on the Brazilian case.

Probably no country in the world currently is as anti-party, both in theory and in practice, as is Brazil. Politicians relate to their party as a *partido de aluguel*, as a rental. They frequently change party, vote against the party line, and refuse any kind of party discipline on the ground that their freedom of representing their constituency cannot be interfered with (see Mainwaring 1991). Thus parties are truly volatile entities; and the Brazilian president is therefore left to float over a vacuum, over an unruly and eminently atomized parliament. Can we expect on this soil that a switch to a parliamentary system would bring about party solidification, and this because in the new system parties would be required to sustain a parliamentary-derived government? This was indeed the argument of the propounders of the referendum (which was defeated). But there is no comparative nor historical evidence that goes to support that expectation.

Compared to the Brazilian parties, the German ones during the Weimar period were 'model parties'; yet their fragmentation was never overcome and their parliamentary performance between 1919–1933 ncither improved nor provided governability. Nothing changed in the behavior or the nature of parties during the Third and Fourth French Republics. The average duration of governments over the forty year period of the Third Republic (1875–1914) was nine months. And the same would apply to pre-fascist Italy. The point is that party solidification and discipline (in parliamentary voting) has never been a feedback of parliamentary government. If a system is assembly-based, atomized, unruly, magmatic, on its own inertia it will remain as it is. I cannot think of any party system that has evolved into a veritable 'system' made of strong, organization-based mass parties on the basis of *internal* parliamentary learning. The metamorphosis from an unstructured to a structured party system has always been triggered by *exogenous* assault and contagion. The earlier parties of notables and of opinion either perished or changed their ways in response to the challenge of externally created (and largely anti-system) mass parties characterized by strong ideological ties and fervor. Now, all the foregoing elements are notably absent in Brazil. Furthermore, the anti-party creed and rhetoric (let alone a typically anti-party electoral legislation) that permeates the country make any kind of parliamentary-fit parties not only unlikely, but altogether inconceivable. The point is, then, that the current Brazilian political culture and tradition nurtures *parliamentary unfit* parties. That under such circumstances a parliamentary experience would lead Brazil out of chaos into some kind of efficient parliamentary government is, in my opinion, against all odds.

On the other hand there are, in Latin America, three major countries that might conceivably afford – in terms of their party system – a switch to parliamentarism, namely, Chile and two-party Argentina and Venezuela. Chile has the most European-like multiparty arrangement of the continent. However, Chile also has a past of 'polarized pluralism', of strong polarization coupled with high party fragmentation. On this background, would it be wise for Chile to adopt a parliamentary system? I doubt it. If Chileans were to decide to abandon their presidential system, they would be well advised, in my opinion, to seek a semi-presidential, not a parliamentary solution.

Argentina is instead a two-party presidential system that currently comes close to enjoying undivided majorities.[20] As a purely conjectural question, would Argentina benefit from a parliamentary transformation? Again, I doubt it. Argentina's parties are not 'solid' parties. What keeps them together and currently brings about their coalescence is the presidential system, that is, the overriding importance of winning a non-divisible prize: the presidency.[21] I would thus expect a different arrangement to bring about a party fragmentation that Argentina does not need. All told, then, Venezuela appears to be the one South American country that can afford – on the basis of its two strong and disciplined parties – to run the risk of a parliamentary experiment. But at the moment the solidity of Venezuela's two-partism appears shattered.[22] I am thus prompted to conclude without further ado that the variety of parliamentarism that would most probably emerge across most of Latin America would be its assemblear variety at its worst.[23]

That presidential systems perform poorly – as Linz maintains (1990, p. 52) – in countries with deep cleavages and with a fragmented party system, is very true. But could they perform better – these conditions remaining equal – under parliamentary forms? *Ceteris paribus* I think not.

NOTES

1. The Irish president truly has very little power, while Austria's and especially Iceland's presidents do have significant power prerogatives which remain, however, a dead letter. The reasons for this will be given *infra* 7.2. Here the point is only that while a direct popular election doubtlessly establishes an independent legitimacy, this constituent factor alone is not, *per se*, of consequence.

2. Duverger classifies them as semi-presidential. Duverger's is, however, a purely legalistic categorization, as he himself admits: 'the concept of a semi-presidential form of government . . . is defined only by the content of the constitution' (1980, p. 166). In due course I shall argue that even this classification is misleading and unacceptable (*infra* 7.2 and 7.3).

3. Thus to speak on the aforesaid grounds of Chile (between 1891 and 1925) and of Peru as parliamentary-like systems is a misclassification leading to serious misperceptions. A similar point is currently raised with regard to Uruguay, but again without merit (or so I contend below, note 11).

4. For other definitions and a discussion, see Shugart and Carey, 1992, pp. 18–22. My definition omits their fourth criterion, namely, that 'the president has some constitutionally granted lawmaking authority'. For me this is too vague to constitute a

criterion, and is already rendered in my criteria. If a president heads/appoints the executive, it goes by itself that he or she has and must have some lawmaking authority. But no harm follows if, *ad abundantiam*, this criterion is added to the three that I propose.

5. The countries in question are listed in my table at p. 174. My listing neglects very small countries and the as yet 'fluid polities' (for reasons explained in Sartori, 1976, ch. 8). It is also too soon to include in the analysis the Eastern European and the formerly Soviet countries exiting from communism. And here I leave aside Mexico, a unique case that I pick up later (*infra* chs. IX and XI).

6. On Mainwaring's counting (1993, pp. 204–7), since at least 1967 there have been, in the world, 31 continuous democracies; of these, only four (Colombia, Costa Rica, the U.S., and Venezuela) have presidential systems. On Riggs's counting (1993, p. 219–20), 'Among 76 open polities, 33 were presidentialist. . . . Their failure rate was far greater than that of the parliamentary system: 91 percent (30 cases) for the former, by contrast with 31 percent (13 cases) for the latter'. To be sure, these statistics cannot prove much without the backing of a rationale.

7. This is more precise than 'mutual independence', for the presidency and congress are not reciprocally independent in all respects.

8. I leave aside how valid Mayhew's findings are. It is notoriously very difficult to appraise qualitatively a legislative output; and Mayhew is also bound to miss the omissions, that is, how many projects are not ever put on the agenda when one knows beforehand that they do not have a shred of a chance. Furthermore, under divided government deals are bound to be struck in one way, and under unified government in another way. In all these respects, and still others, I consider Mayhew's evidence suspect and highly unconvincing. But if Mayhew were right, my argument would be reinforced.

9. The divide is, here, whether a president can negotiate deals with congressional party leaders that can thereafter deliver their votes, versus the extent to which deals have to be negotiated with members of Congress on a one-by-one basis.

10. However, in 1992 and 1993 Venezuela (which stands out, not only in duration but also in terms of economic affluence, as one of the most 'solid' Latin American democracies) witnessed –

much to everybody's dismay – two military coup attempts; and Peru has stumbled into some 18 months of unconstitutional rule. To wit, President Fujimori staged in April 1992 an *autogolpe*, a self-coup, and has governed with emergency powers and military backing until he narrowly won, on October 31, 1993, a referendum for a new constitution (which allows him, inter alia, to run for re-election) drafted by a Constituent Congress somewhat dubiously elected in November 1992.

11. Uruguay has displayed uncharacteristic constitutional oscillations between 'quasi-presidentialism' (1830, 1934, 1942, 1966) and not (1918, 1952), but I would definitely consider its present-day system (following the 1973 coup and the 1973–84 interruption) a presidential one. That the legislature may censure ministers and that the President is empowered to dissolve the legislature represent a deviation from the United States model but does not contradict my defining criteria of presidentialism (*supra* 5.1) and hardly affects the substance.

12. Ecuador is in near permanent crisis; Bolivia has undergone, between 1952 and 1982, some seventeen military interventions; Honduras and Guatemala perform messily and largely under de facto military control; and the Dominican Republic is more a *dictablanda* than anything else.

13. Mrs. Aquino came to power in 1986 only because 'people power' in the streets of Manila (assisted by U.S. persuasion) forced Marcos to flee. Thus the election of President Ramos in 1992 was the first free, regular transmission of power in 26 years. And while Mrs. Aquino was a somewhat symbolic president 'by acclamation', Ramos is an outsider (a former general) with little and certainly inadequate parliamentary support.

14. This matter will be analyzed and discussed *infra* 11.2, for I have still to establish how presidentialism relates to multiparty situations and/or to party atomization.

15. All these points are covered in detail *infra* ch. X.

16. For instance, Chile's constitution of 1989 empowers the president to dissolve the Chamber of Deputies (article 32, sect. 5). Since I have already discussed (*supra* 5.2) how this 'anomaly' affects the division of power principle, here the point only is that reinforcing the presidential prerogatives is a matter of concern.

17. This mood shows, e.g., in the proposal put forward in Venezuela to submit presidents to popular recall.

18. In this respect the Chilean case with Allende is emblematic. As Mainwaring (1993, p. 208) sums it up, 'in Chile in 1973 opponents of the Popular Unity government feared that by allowing Allende to complete his six year term (1970–1976) they would open the door to authoritarian socialism. Allende had lost the support of the majority of the legislature, and in a parliamentary system he would have been voted out of office. In a presidential system, however, there was no way of replacing him except for a coup'. The generalization thus resulting is that 'in many cases, a coup appears to be the only means of getting rid of an incompetent or unpopular president'.

19. Linz also concurs with Lijphart's criticism that presidentialism is tainted by a majoritarian bent. But this is a dubious point; and I certainly do not subscribe to Lijphart's anti-majoritarian obsession (*supra* 4.4). In my opinion, proportional politics can be as damaging, to say the very least, as majoritarian politics.

20. President Alfonsin had a slight majority, in 1983–87, in the Chamber of Deputies, but not in the Senate; and President Menem had, since 1989 and during his tenure, a majority in the Senate, but not (if unassisted) in the low chamber. This is not, then, a clear cut status of undivided majority. Historically, and aside from the Perons' periods, only President Frondizi (1958–62) had a majority in both houses of Congress.

21. The Radical and Peronist parties do have a 'centralist' tradition; even so, as the Peronist party loses and indeed dismisses the doctrine of its founder, I would say that the presidential factor becomes weightier as the ideological differences between the two parties lose weight. But I do not hold, with this, that the presidential prize is a sufficient condition – either in Argentina or elsewhere – for two-partism.

22. Reference is made to the December 1993 presidential election won by the independent Caldera with the support of 17 political groups, and against the two parties – the socialdemocratic Democratic Action, and the socialchristian COPEI – that had been in control since 1958. Let it also be noted that Caldera will be a minority president

23. For an assessment of the various levels of 'institutionalization' (or not) of parties across Latin America see Mainwaring and Scully eds., 1994, esp. ch. 1.

6 Parliamentary Systems

6.1 TYPES OF PARLIAMENTARISM

Parliamentary systems owe their name to their founding principle, namely, that parliament is sovereign. Thus parliamentary systems do not permit a separation of power between parliament and government: they are all based on legislative-executive power sharing.[1] Which is also to say that all the systems that we call parliamentary require governments to be appointed, supported and, as the case may be, discharged, by parliamentary vote. But to say that governments are parliament-supported is not saying much. It does not even begin to explain why the polities in question display strong or feeble government, stability or instability, effectiveness or immobilism and, in sum, good, or mediocre, or even detestable performances.

The fact is that 'parliamentarism' does not denote a single entity. If the performances of parliamentary systems are as different as they are, this is because they relate to, and result from, very different kinds of executive-legislative linkage. Indeed, there are at least three major varieties of parliamentary systems: at one extreme the English-type of premiership or cabinet system, in which the executive forcefully prevails over parliament; at the other extreme the French (III and IV Republic) type of assembly government that makes governing a near-impossibility; and a middle-of-the-way formula of party-controlled parliamentarism.

So, parliamentarism may fail us just as much and as easily as presidentialism. If we wish to argue that the former is better than the latter, we must immediately declare *which parliamentarism* is chosen, and see to it that the exit from pure presidentialism does not simply lead – along a path of least resistance – to pure parliamentarism, that is, to assembly government and misgovernment.

The specifics of each parliamentary form will be outlined in the next sections. But the underlying, common problem of all parliamentarism is to have parties that do not cross, in voting on the floor of the Houses, party lines. While in the American case party indiscipline may be an asset, in the parliamentary case party indiscipline is always and necessarily a liability. Parliamentary-fit parties – as I have called them – are, to begin with, parties that hold together in supporting the government (generally a coalition) that is their appointee.

Therefore the understanding of parliamentarism assumes an understanding of who controls the parties, how, and – in turn – what it is that parties control. This is no simple and easy inquiry, and will be pursued in this work at various points (but see especially *infra* 12.2). It should be clear from the outset, however, that in this inquiry we must always assess if the 'real unit' is the party, or its fractions and factions, or otherwise if both the party and sub-party units have lost their centrality.

6.2   POWER SHARING

Parliamentary systems, I have noted, are all power-sharing systems. But power sharing cannot be pinned down as tidily as power division can. The formula is elusive, for sharing denotes diffusion and diffuseness. Who shares what, with whom, in what way or to what extent? To say the least, power sharing admits a very great variance. Still some order can be brought into this maze by looking into the core authority structure in which a chief executive, a prime minister, is empowered to perform. From this standpoint the head of government may relate to the members of his government as:

  i) a first *above unequals*
 ii) a first *among unequals*
iii) a first *among equals*.

The former are all power sharing formulas in that they all exclude a power concentration in just one person, in a *primus solus,* as in the case of the American President whose government is only his private cabinet. But they are indeed very different formulas. A British prime minister stands as a *primus* (first) above unequals, for he or she truly runs the government and has a free hand in picking and firing truly 'subordinate' ministers; the German Chancellor is less pre-eminent but still is a *primus* among unequals (not among equals); whereas a prime minister in an ordinary parliamentary system is a *primus inter pares,* among equals, and thus not much of a *primus* either. We can, of course, bicker about the nuances. Nonetheless, the criterion that underpins the three formulas is neat enough.

A first *above unequals* is a chief executive that is the party leader, that can hardly be unseated by a parliamentary vote, and that appoints and changes cabinet ministers at his or her pleasure. So, this 'first' rules over its ministers and indeed overrules them. A first *among unequals* may not be the official party leader, and yet cannot be unseated by a mere no-confidence parliamentary vote and is expected to remain in office even when his cabinet members change. So, this 'first' can unseat its ministers but cannot be unseated by them. Finally, a first *among equals* is a prime minister that falls with his cabinet, that generally must embark on the governmental team 'imposed' ministers, and that has little control over the team (better described as a non-team whose untouchables play their own game).

The significant point is that the formulas in question outline a scale of power sharing arrangements that undercut the conventional wisdom about what presidentialism and parliamentarism, respectively, do best. For one, the scale indicates that an English prime minister can govern far more effectively than an American president.[2] This entails that the presidential *primus solus* formula cannot be credited with any prevailing 'governing merit'. Furthermore, the scale suggests that there is no net advantage in replacing a *primus solus,* a president, with a *primus inter pares.* Indeed, a prime minister that cannot control his ministers (for he cannot fire them), and that does not even have a free hand in choosing them, cannot be expected to be really in charge.

So, the power sharing formulas that hold 'governing promise' are i) first above unequals, and ii) first among unequals. This is the same as suggesting that the interesting working cases of parliamentary government are the premiership systems that range from England to Germany. But this is by no means to assert that all other forms of parliamentarism are non-working. In the next two sections we shall explore, then, the conditions that explain and sustain the performance of all the parliamentary systems that perform.

6.3   PREMIERSHIP SYSTEMS

The premiership system, or cabinet system, at its best is best illustrated by the English system of government.[3] As everyone knows, the English premiership system assumes single party government (it would founder with coalition government), which in turn assumes a single member district system that engenders a two-party system. Let it also be underscored that it is single party government that calls for the strict party discipline that obtains in Westminster, for here to vote against one's own government would imply handing it over to the opposition.[4]

The above indicates that the Westminster system of government rests on three major conditions. I further suggest that these conditions build on each other in this order: i) plurality elections, ii) two-partism, iii) strong partisan discipline.[5] This implies that if the first condition is altered, a domino effect will follow – a point that seemingly escapes the British scholars and politicians that press for the adoption of some kind of PR system and, in any case, for the rejection of the winner-take-all system.

So, the English premiership system can be easily destroyed while, on the other hand, is not easily obtainable. Remember, on this score, that for my laws on the effects of electoral systems (*supra* 3.3 and 3.4) plurality elections cannot produce a two-party system unless the incoercible third party electorates happen to be dispersed nation-wide at below-plurality levels –

a hard condition for newcomers to meet. Therefore any country that adopts a single member district system on the argument that a premiership system of government would follow, may be severely disappointed. Remember, also, that the winner-take-all system is inadvisable when a polity is polarized and/or characterized by a heterogeneous political culture (*supra* 4.2).

Moving on, while the United Kingdom and the English-modeled countries illustrate the strong case of premiership parliamentarism, Germany illustrates the weak, or weaker case of the category. The German Federal Republic has never had a two-party system (even counting, as I do, the CDU and the Bavarian CSU as one party), and only for a short time single-party government. It has long been, instead, a three-party system (some say a two-and-a-half), has always displayed two-member coalition governments, and does not employ a majoritarian electoral system. Furthermore, the German chancellor is elected in and by parliament and is not in any formal – legally formal – way the leader of his party. Even so, the German *Kanzlerdemokratie*, their Chancellor-centered practice of government, can well be classified among the premiership systems.

Do the differences between the English and German arrangements suggest that a premiership system is not necessarily based on the leadership principle? Yes and no, I would say. Because German parties do indicate to the electorate, at election time, their would-be chancellor (thus infringing, or at least enfeebling, the parliamentary principle). But we cannot make too much of this. For the electoral pre-designation of the prime minister makes sense with a party system (be it of two or two-and-a-half parties) that allows for only two credible contenders; but makes far less sense with multi-party systems that require extended (more-than-two) party coalitions, and makes no sense at all when extended coalition governments contain parties of near-equal strength. Under these conditions, the prime minister is necessarily part and parcel of the coalition negotiations, and cannot be 'promised' in advance. A further point is this: that the electoral pre-designation of the prime ministers should not be mistaken with the utterly different proposal of having a popularly, directly elected prime minister (a proposal currently adopted in Israel, and aired in Italy, Japan and the Netherlands).[6]

How did the German premiership system come about? The factors and reasons that explain the German *Kanzlerdemokratie* are, I submit, i) the outlawing of the anti-system parties, ii) the *Sperrklausel*, iii) the so-called constructive vote of no confidence – in that order. And let me begin by explaining why the first reason is indeed 'first'.

Many, if not most observers, hold that the German three-party system results from the 5 percent clause of exclusion, from the *Sperrklausel*, in combination with a mixed (half-majoritarian) electoral system. All of this is clearly wrong. The German electoral system obtains an almost pure proportional representation (*supra* 2.2), and a 5 percent threshold is unlikely to downsize anywhere – Germany included – the format of any party system to three parties. So, the beginning of the German political system is not in its electoral system but in the circumstance that judicial decisions have fundamentally altered the 'natural development' of the party system. The Karlsruhe constitutional court outlawed in 1953 the neo-Nazi Socialist Reich party, and in 1956 the Communist party; and had this not happened, the German three-party system would not have happened either. And I call the above a circumstance to underscore that constitutional structures had nothing to do with this momentous happening. Note, also, that the judicial decisions in question were particularly 'circumstantial' in that they clearly belonged to the climate of the Fifties and, furthermore, to the specific context which justified them. Could they be repeated in any present-day established democracy? I doubt it.

So, the outlawing of the anti-system parties comes first in the strong sense that it provides the other two factors with a leverage that in themselves they do not have. Enough has been already said of the *Sperrklausel*. We must pause instead on the third factor – the constructive vote of no-confidence – which also happens to be the specifically constitutional element of *Kanzlerdemokratie*. The provision says that a chancellor cannot be unseated by a no-confidence parliamentary vote unless and until his successor has been nominated. While this constitutional device is not an insuperable obstacle, its efficacy should not be sneezed at, for it is far easier to assemble a negative majority, a majority that simply ousts a government, than to bring together a positive majority that also agrees on the new chancellor.[7]

The comparison between the British and German ways of establishing a premiership system was left earlier at noting that the German leadership principle appeared to have weaker foundations than the English ones. However, it must now be noted that this weakness is corrected by the constructive vote of no-confidence. And an additional reinforcement to the German premiership system comes from the fact that parliament appoints only the chancellor, not – as in most parliamentary systems – the full government. A procedure that establishes that the premier stands above his government, that he or she definitely is, as I said earlier, a first *among unequals*.

We can now confront the question of which of the two models is easier to copy. In the countries that are unhappy about their parliamentary democracy and are seeking to amend their ways, the prevailing wisdom is that the German model is the more accessible one, the model that lends itself to relatively easy imitation. But my analysis leads to the opposite conclusion. The English system is largely constitution-made, the German system is largely circumstance-made; and, surely, structures lend themselves to replication better than circumstances (in the meaning just explained). If we opt for the Westminster model, all we have to do is to adopt the winner-take-all electoral system; and if we are lucky, that is to say, if the electorate happens to be 'normally distributed' across the constituencies, the rest of the set-up follows in part by itself, and can be otherwise handled by constitutional intervention.

But if we opt for the German model, what is it that we have to do? As we know, the adoption of the *Sperrklausel* would not do the job, for it would not, by itself, downsize the party system to the point at which it needs to be downsized for a premiership system to emerge. So, how do we do it? While we cannot expect to be assisted by constitutional court surgery, we can, of course, renounce PR and pass to a plurality electoral system. If so, however, we are on the more painful English track, and no longer on the painless German one. Let it be added, as a further note of caution, that the German system itself, as it has been until the middle of the Nineties, may well be on the wane.[8] Assume that the West–East German unification will in due course raise the party format of the country to four–five parties. Would the German *Kanzlerdemokratie* still perform under these circumstances? Probably not. For the strength of the chancellor does not extend beyond his own party. This delimitation is of no consequence until the second partner of the German coalitions, the FDP, is 6 to 7 times smaller. On this ratio, the Liberal party can neither aspire to the chancellorship nor condition its choice; it can only cause the fall of a Socialist or Christian-Democratic dominated coalition government. Suppose now that two additional parties become relevant, and thus that future coalitions will have to include at least three parties of near-equal, or at any rate of less unequal strength. Under these conditions the German-type premiership system becomes inoperative, for its remaining pillars – the 'lonely' election in parliament and the constructive vote of no-confidence – could not possibly suffice to sustain it.

6.4   WORKING PARLIAMENTARISM

Does the conclusion that the premiership systems cannot be easily reproduced lead to the ulterior conclusion that 'working parliamentarism' is and will remain a rare event? Of course not. With reference to governing capabilities, 'working' branches out in two meanings, namely, effective government and/or stable government; and this distinction allows for three combinations, that is, a government that is: i) both effective and stable, ii) stable and possibly effective, iii) unstable. And this framework allows for an array of working cases that certainly extends beyond the English model and the German experience.

The first combination eminently includes the premiership systems, but also includes the 'predominant party system' of countries such as Sweden and Norway (for long stretches since the Thirties), Japan (between 1954 and 1993) and Spain (as of 1982), which may neither have premiership structures nor a two–three party format, and yet display uninterruptedly for some ten to as much as forty years, single-party government (of the same party) – and this on account of the simple fact that one party obtains, across a succession of legislatures, the absolute majority of parliamentary seats.[9] Predominant party systems thus provide the stability and the effectiveness capability that all single-party governments provide – even though in this pattern duration and efficiency may not correlate positively, for countries without alternative government (or too little of it) lack the stimulations brought about by two-party rotations in office.

The point is that what cannot be accomplished on the basis of the leadership principle can be accomplished by a particular structuring of the party system. That is also to say that the list of the working parliamentary democracies is extended by cases that are no longer explained by any particular constitutional arrangement. Beyond this frontier we can still find, to be sure, multi-party countries with coalition governments that turn out to be stable and reasonably effective. But these are single-country success stories whose success must be credited to policies and personal leadership qualities, not to any kind of structure. Provided that one crucial condition is always respected, namely, that the parties are parliamentary-fit and thus sufficiently controllable and in control.

Can a general conclusion be drawn as to why parliamentary democracies can and do work? The answer that emerges from our overview is that parliamentary government works (works better) when its name is somewhat of a misnomer, that is to say, when parliament does *not* govern, when it is muzzled. Conversely put, working parliamentarism never is a 'pure' parliamentarism that fully embodies the principle of the sovereignty of parliament. Rather, parliamentarism works when its wings are clipped, when it acquires – we could say – a semi-parliamentary form. Somewhat paradoxically, the less a government is truly parliamentary, the better it performs.

6.5   ASSEMBLY GOVERNMENT

Countries that exit from a dictatorship may well have little choice other than the parliamentary one. But the people discontented with presidential systems that are offered to choose, in its stead, a parliamentary system should be alerted to its perils. Yet the eulogists of parliamentarism seldom acknowledge its dark sides. Read this summation of how they perceive their protégé:

> Those who have been frustrated with the stalemates of the American system . . . have looked longingly across the Atlantic . . . and admired the streamlined unity of other democratic governments . . . In the parliamentary democracies the legislative majority is sovereign, and a committee of that majority – the cabinet – both leads the legislature and directs the executive. Power is unified. Responsibility is clearly fixed. Strong party discipline assures prime ministers and their cabinets that they normally can act quickly and decisively . . . In two-party parliamentary systems, of which Great Britain is the prototype, votes of nonconfidence are rare . . . In the multiparty parliamentary systems of the European continent, governments are usually formed by coalitions . . . [but] as long as they can resolve disagreements . . . within their cabinets they are as certain of legislative support as are the governments of Britain. Under any of these parliamentary systems, governments can be formed, in Lloyd Cutler's phrase. They can act. They can speak . . . with a single, clear voice.[10]   *Sundquist*

As the above well reveals, the telescope of the eulogist of parliamentarism only sees as far as England and goes blank as it reaches the Channel at Dover. The parliamentary experience of continental Europe is just recalled as a somewhat imperfect reflection of the English teaching; and the assemblear kind of parliamentarism passes unnoticed and unmentioned. It might be argued that our eulogists miss assemblearism not because they know nothing about it, but because they consider it a deviation, a degenerative form. But no. If the founding principle of all parliamentary systems is that parliament is sovereign, then assembly government represents the direct lineage of that principle. Let alone that assembly-centered governing represents the 'natural' path of development of the parliamentary principle: it comes by itself, on its own inertia.

The prototype of assembly government has been the French Third Republic, the aptly called 'republic of deputies'. But, e.g., the French Fourth Republic and Italy escaped it only to the extent that parliamentary 'partycracy' (*partitocrazia*, i.e. party power) kept it at bay. Currently most post-communist parliamentary experiences are of the assemblear variety. And I would expect most Latin-American democracies (if they were to abandon their presidential forms) to fall straight into assemblearism. As for its characteristics, they can be quickly derived from our previous quotation by replacing its plusses with minuses. In the assemblear pattern i) the cabinet does not lead the legislature; ii) power is not unified but scattered and atomized; iii) responsibility vanishes altogether; iv) party discipline goes from poor to non-existent; v) prime ministers and their cabinets cannot act quickly and decisively; vi) coalitions seldom resolve their disagreements and are always uncertain of legislative support; and vii) governments can never act and speak with a single, clear voice.

All of the above does not need at this stage of the argument any particular explanation, but for this one point: why governments are shot down with gusto every year or less. After all – so runs the perplexity – even when governments are coalitions they still represent, for their supporters, 'their government'. Not really, however. For in most instances a coalition government that falls is replaced by another coalition government of the same parties. Therefore killing one's own government is not – as in England – giving the government away, but giving oneself a chance of entering the cabinet. For an MP in waiting, cabinet instability is a career opener.[11] But then, does cabinet instability really matter?

6.6   STABILITY AND EFFECTIVENESS

In much of the literature 'stability' is *the* major indicator of
working democracy. The reasoning is that if a parliamentary
system obtains stable government, then it equally obtains
effective government. Conversely, unstable governments attest
to inefficient government. But this reasoning stands up to
scrutiny only in part.

Let us begin with 'governability', effectiveness or efficiency
in governing. The preliminary admonishment is that these
notions do not address actual performances but *structural
capabilities*. Performances depend on performers just as driv-
ing depends on drivers.[12] However, drivers need roads and,
similarly, performers need structures that allow them to
perform. So, we cannot get decisive government without a
decisive prime minister; but even a decisive prime minister
cannot be decisive if the decision-making machinery is
clogged and works against him. A second point is this: that
we should not confuse 'effective government' with 'activist
government'. The former is a government that has the
capacity of implementing the policies that it pursues; but it
may expound a non-activist philosophy of government and
therefore choose, whenever it so decides, to remain inactive.
The difference between effective and impotent government is
that the former may decide against doing something, whereas
the latter cannot do what it would like to do. In parallel
fashion the difference between effective and activist government is that while the first may be effective in undoing and
dismantling things, an activist government is assumed to be a
'doer' for it assumes that there is no problem that politics
cannot solve.

Even so, a government empowered to perform worries a
number of people. We favor efficient government on the
presumption that it will govern well. But if we assume or
fear governments that misgovern, then the less they can
govern, the better. The third point thus is that inefficient
government is the best defense we have against bad government: the lesser its effectiveness, the lesser the harm.

I will not deny that this argument has a point – but not a crushing one. To begin with, inefficient government too can be quite harmful, for one of the major characteristics of inefficiency is to waste resources, to use resources that do not achieve any end, that simply go down the drain. But above all my sense is that we are increasingly entering a bewilderingly complex and fragile artificial world that cannot 'naturally' save itself by itself (nor, indeed, save itself from itself). Whether we like it or not, the invisible hand can no longer perform unassisted by the visible one, by governments that intervene and interfere. I concede that the badness of bad government may be lessened by ineffective government. But I do not concede that we can afford gridlocked, immobilist and impotent governments. Effective government is a risk that we must take – if for no better reason, by default, because the alternatives are worse.

Turning to 'stability', the introductory question is: which stability, or who's stability? *Stable democracy* (i.e., regime stability) is one thing, *stable government* quite another thing. Yet we often allow the glitter of stable democracy to enshrine stable government. This is, however, an undue extrapolation. That democracy should not fall is obviously important. But why is it important that governments should not fall? The answer generally is that stable government 'indicates' effective government. Alas, no. Government stability stands for a mere *duration*; and governments can be both long lived and impotent: their time duration is by no means an indicator and even less an activator of efficiency or efficacy. Indeed, in most parliamentary systems which require government by coalition, governments prolong their survival by doing next to nothing. In this context the little that coalition governments can do is usually done in the first six months, in the initial honeymoon period in which they cannot be decently overthrown. After that, they are left to gain time by staying still, by trying not to rock the boat. Thus the problem is not longevity, how long governments last, but whether governments are given the capacity to govern. Stable government may be a facilitating condition, but is certainly not a *sufficient condition* of effective government.

After having firmed up that a government can be stable *and* idle, long lasting *and* powerless, it can of course be conceded that duration helps the implementation of policies. However, the more we hold that stable government is a necessary (though not sufficient) condition of efficient government, the more we must make sure that a stable government is true to its name and indicates a *same* government that lasts. We are being told, instead, that unstable governments can be stable ones in disguise, that 'apparent instability' is only appearance when the underlying reality is one of substantive continuity. The argument thus becomes that unstable (short-lived) governments are as good as stable ones, as long as the political personnel that rotates in office is roughly the same (unchanging). Well, no – I disagree.

If, as I have argued, governmental stability is per se a misdirected concern, then the notion of 'personnel stability' (in government) is an equally misdirected remedy. I would further add that the argument is flawed and that by endorsing it we just make matters worse. The honorable Eternity (his proper name, mind you) has been – we read in his record – seven times Prime Minister and has otherwise or in the intervals occupied cabinet positions for some forty years as, for example, Minister of Foreign Affairs, of Defense, of Education, of Interior, and more. Wonderful for him – his personal stability in office is indisputable. But in what way is his personal stability a system-serving one, a stability that benefits the polity? In no way, I would say. Indeed, by endlessly dropping whatever expertise he may have acquired along the way, the honorable Eternity disseminates all around the discontinuity (not the continuity) of his unending incompetence. And the reason that makes the honorable Eternity an everlasting Minister in everything is precisely that he well knows that his cabinet staying power has nothing to do with his performance in office (nor, incidentally, with his natural intelligence), and everything to do with his intra-party factional strength and maneuverings. And if this is what 'substantial stability' truly stands for, then I submit that we are better off without it.

6.7 THE DIRECTLY ELECTED PREMIER

Thus far I have discussed duration as an ill-focussed concern and a misleading priority. But it becomes worse than that when we encounter the already mentioned proposal (*supra* 6.3) of a direct, popular election of the prime minister for the entire duration of a legislature. Since the proposal does not concern itself with how this stable, 'enduring' prime minister is assured of obtaining an equally durable parliamentary support, it is apparent that here duration becomes a fetish. We elect a general without giving him soldiers, and we assume that he will win his battles because he cannot be removed from office. Does that make any sense? Not to me.

The one country that has adopted the direct election of the prime minister (for four years) is, to date, Israel. This provision will go into effect with the next Knesset election scheduled for mid-1996, but was entered in the Basic Law in 1992. It does not provide the prime minister with a majority (this problem is totally neglected); it simply gives him the stick of dissolving parliament.[13] It is not much of a stick either, for a premier that sends the Knesset home also dismisses itself, and any dissolution of the Knesset entails his own fall. Now, a small country with a population in the order of five million (less than New York City) can perhaps afford incessant elections. Even so, there is no assurance that re-electing a parliament will produce a different parliament, whereas it is quite certain that a country in epidemic electoral fever, that is, persistently keyed to actual or potential electoral politics, will deliver bad politics. On the other hand, why should a parliament play the game of voting out of office the prime minister? It can play the very different game of upholding him or her at the votes of confidence while obstructing across the board his legislation.

One of the advocates of this reform, Bogdanor, writes: 'Direct election of the prime minister will give Israel a system of government bearing marked resemblances to that of the French Fifth Republic' (in Sprinzak and Diamond, 1993, p. 97). But we shall see in the next chapter that this is quite wrong. The French semi-presidential system characteristically allows for a prime minister that always commands a parliamentary majority (and that can be changed as this majority changes). Instead the directly elected prime minister cannot be changed and remains stuck with the support or non-support that he is given by the electorate. Bogdanor argues that the directly elected premier should be chosen before the parliamentary election, so that the electorate knows how to vote if it wishes to elect a majority supporting the prime minister (ibid., pp. 98–99). This is very unconvincing. American voters do not create a divided government because they vote in the dark without knowing who will be elected president, but deliberately split their ticket. On the other hand, the chances that in fragmented multiparty countries like Israel, Italy and the Netherlands a coattail effect would boost the elected prime minister's party to absolute majority levels range from very poor to zero.

I must also disagree, I am afraid, with Bogdanor's underplaying of the divided majority impasse. Minority governments do frequently arise in parliamentary systems (they are almost the rule in Denmark)[14] but they result from, and stand upon, negotiations with the more or less variable parliamentary majorities that do in fact keep them in office. Any analogy with parliamentary minority governments entirely breaks down, then, when referred to a minority premier that can neither be negotiated nor overturned. To argue, therefore, that a Knesset controlled by the opposition simply entails and means 'checking the power of the prime minister' (ibid., p. 99) is, to say the least, a grand understatement.[15]

While it is mistaken to assimilate the directly elected prime minister to a semi-presidential, French-like, arrangement, it is equally mistaken to assimilate it to presidentialism.[16] I have already indicated that the direct election of a president does not suffice to create a presidential system (see *supra* 5.1). Furthermore the prime minister in question is still subject to parliamentary confidence or non-confidence votes; his major power resource is the typical one of parliamentary systems, namely, the dissolution of the legislature; and while presidents are generally allowed various veto, extraordinary and emergency powers, this armory does not accompany the direct election of the prime minister. The one and only analogy bewteen elected premier and elected president resides in a common drawback, namely, the rigidity in or of office. A president that becomes enormously unpopular, or that is disastrously incompetent, or that patently and menacingly oversteps his powers, cannot be replaced (impeachment aside) for the duration of his tenure. The directly elected prime minister either governs by dissolving parliament, or introduces the same rigidity and the same drawback in a non-presidential system, that is, where the nature of the system does not require it.

So, the direct election of a premier is not a sort of *ersatz*, of substitute, for a presidential arrangement. If one desires presidentialism, one must redesign the entire mechanism. *Per contra*, the insertion of a non-removeable, popularly elected premier into a parliamentary system is like entering a stone into an engine. If it doesn't break it, it must be a very strong engine.

NOTES

1. Note that power sharing does not entail that parliamentary systems are systems of 'mutual dependence' between parliament and government. The premise that parliament is sovereign rules out a reciprocal dependence, that is, a veritable interdependence between legislative and executive bodies. The power of dissolving parliament cannot be put on a par with the parliamentary power over government. The first is a sporadic possibility, the second is a continuous control over every piece of legislation. Furthermore, the power of dissolution generally is (England aside) a prerogative of the head of state, not of the prime minister.

2. In the counting of Polsby (1993, p. 31) 'In their last couple of years in office, Republican Presidents Eisenhower, Nixon, Ford, Reagan and Bush all had to deal with Democratic Congresses and all got their way about half the time they took positions on bills. . . . Earlier in their terms they usually scored two-thirds or better.' Even so, no British prime minister has

ever seen its bills defeated in parliament on a 1 to 3 or even 1 to 2 ratio.

3. I use here the two labels interchangeably, though it is self-evident that 'premiership system' suggests a strong preeminence, while 'cabinet system' emphasizes the collegial aspect. As of recently, the Conservatives have accentuated the premiership configuration, while since 1981 the Labor party statutes restrict the power of its leader by requiring him to bring into his government the shadow cabinet of the opposition period. These differences and over time shifts are immaterial, however, for the point that parliament is executive-controlled.

4. To be sure, the Westminster back-benchers do not always have the party whip over their shoulders and are permitted some 'free voting'. But when it matters the prime minister can and does override any within-party opposition, until and unless it comes to issues – such as England's entry into Europe – that deeply and fundamentally tear, in one, each party and the country itself.

5. I omit the party leadership element, in part because I propose to probe this point later in connection with the German case.

6. I have strong reservations about this device; but here I simply underscore that the direct election of a prime minister is based on a false witnessing, for neither England nor Germany can be called upon to endorse it. My objection is spelled out *infra*, 6.7.

7. In fact, to date there has been only one instance, in 1982, of a parliamentary change of chancellor (from the Social-Democratic Schmidt to the Christian-Democrat Kohl), which resulted from the break-up of the Liberal–SPD coalition.

8. Note, in this connection, that the Greens and the *Republikaner* are already able to pass the 5 percent barrier, and are in fact breaking up the three-party format at the *Länder* level. The autumn 1994 general elections of unified Germany may well harbor a shake-up.

9. The literature often confuses a predominant party *system* with the dominant *party*, which is only a party that enjoys a comfortable relative majority over the others. For instance, Italy's DC (Christian-Democracy) has uninterruptedly been for some 40 years – but for the initial 1948 legislature – a dominant party, and no predominant pattern has ever followed. The same is true for Israel's Mapai, its major socialist party, which has been until 1977 the dominant party at the Knesset. I deal extensively with this distinction in Sartori, 1976, pp. 192–201; but much of the profession does not grasp, it

would appear, the critical importance of distinguishing a single party from systemic properties.

10. The quote is from Sundquist, 1992, pp. 18–19, but does not represent, I should underscore, his own view.

11. The argument that an MP that fails to support the government of which his party is a coalition member, jeopardizes his own re-election holds only in the rare event that his re-election is controlled by a strongly unified party, and also assumes a roll-call vote. But governments are often crippled under the cloak of secret voting.

12. Structuralism, or the structural approach to politics, is assumed to hold that leadership and choice play a minor role, if any, in affecting outcomes. It should be clear by now that my understanding of structuralism is very different. In this work much of my argument is structural and yet I hold that outcomes are decided by leadership and choice.

13. More exactly, a no-confidence vote of the Knesset to the prime minister itself and/or to his government automatically entails its dissolution and new elections. The prime minister is also entitled to dissolve the Knesset on his or her initiative, provided that the President concurs.

14. See Strom 1990, and Daalder 1971. Note that many minority cabinets are such in appearance, not in substance, while this would never be the case with a directly elected prime minister confronted by an opposition that holds the majority.

15. The understatement is, once again, based on the misstatement that in the event the political system would move to 'periods of cohabitation or power sharing, similar to the system in France between 1986 and 1988'. I must insist that this is wrong. In France between 1986–88 it was the president, Mitterrand, that lost his majority; but the prime minister, Chirac, was a majority supported premier. The same applies to 1993, when Mitterrand found himself once again obliged to appoint a non-socialist, majority based prime minister.

16. See e.g. Shugart and Carey, 1992, p. 164: in 'proposals . . . featuring the direct election of the prime minister . . . the elected head of government would be a president by our definition'. Since the authors specifically indicate that 'the prime minister would be permitted to dissolve the assembly, but then she or he would have to stand concurrently for reelection', I fail to see how this feature squares with any definition of presidentialism.

7   Semi-Presidentialism

7.1   THE FRENCH PROTOTYPE

It has been seen that both presidentialism and parliamentarism may fail us, especially in their pure forms. It is from both these ends, then, that we are prompted to seek a 'mixed' solution, a political form that stands at the cross-roads between presidential and parliamentary systems and draws from both. This mixed form has come to be known – I think tellingly – as semi-presidentialism.[1] While we should not read the label too literally, it does convey that it is from the vantage point of presidentialism, not from the vantage point of parliamentarism, that our mixed system is best understood and construed. For the argument flows more cogently from the top down than from the parliamentary base up.

The common denominator of both presidentialism and semi-presidentialism is a popularly elected president or, at a minimum, a president that is *not* elected in and by parliament. But beyond this common foundation the two forms radically depart from one another, for semi-presidentialism is 'semi' precisely in that it halves presidentialism by substituting a dual authority structure to a monocentric authority structure. In presidential systems the president is protected and insulated from parliamentary interference by the division of power principle. Instead, semi-presidential systems perform on a power sharing basis: the president must share power with a prime minister; and, in turn, the prime minister must obtain continuous parliamentary support.

Does the above suffice to define semi-presidentialism? Very definitely the answer is no. But for the time being this matter must rest. With reference to presidentialism it is permissible to start with the definition because the form obtains an undisputed prototype – the U.S. presidency – and has consolidated itself into a well identifiable pattern across a sizeable number of countries. But with reference to semi-presidentialism we must be aware of, and steer clear from, an egg–chicken circularity. On the one hand, we do not agree on the countries that qualify as being semi-presidential; and the obvious reason for this is that we lack a definition. On the other hand, how can we define the specimen unless we know from which countries its defining characteristics are to be inferred? The way out is to stipulate that the category obtains an extant case – which doubtlessly is the French Fifth Republic – and to pick up the matter from here.

The one characteristic that any semi-presidentialism *must* have (by virtue of its very name) is a dual authority structure, a two-headed configuration. Thus any semi-presidential constitution must establish, in some manner, a dyarchy between a president, the head of state, and a prime minister that heads the government. In the 1958 French constitution the premier's 'head' is clearly outlined in articles 20 and 21, which read, respectively, that 'The government determines and directs the national policies', and that 'The prime minister directs the actions of the government.' The presidential 'head' is outlined, instead, far less clearly and in a more scattered manner in articles 11, 12, 15, 16 and 52 of the constitution; and this scattering corresponds to the fact that the 'principal powers of the president . . . have a spasmodic character. . . . They are not normal prerogatives . . . but exceptional powers which can be used only infrequently. Furthermore [most presidential powers] are not powers of decision. They tend either to prevent a decision . . . or to submit the decision to the French people (dissolution, referendum)'.[2] What is very clear, then, is that the intent of the drafter of the constitution, Michel Debré, was not to establish a preeminent, 'imperial' president.

However, in this case more than in others the living or, as the Italian wording has it, the 'material' constitution has quickly taken precedence over the 'formal' one. It is also mistaken to derive the French semi-presidential system only from the 1958 text of the constitution, for the actual configuration of the system was crucially determined, in 1962, by a new element: the direct, popular election of the president. The French model results, then, from a 1958 constitution whose balance was tipped in 1962, and whose practice was established by the initial, pacesetting presidency of general De Gaulle.[3] And after some 30 years of running what the French actually have is, in essence, a bicephalous, two-headed system whose heads are *unequal* but also *in oscillation* among themselves. More exactly put, the 'first head' is by custom (the conventions of the constitutions) the president, by law (the written text of the constitution) the prime minister, and the oscillations reflect the respective majority status of one over the other.

On this last note we are brought back to the American problem of 'divided government' (*supra* 5.2). Presidential systems cannot easily cope, we know, with split majorities. The crucial question thus becomes whether semi-presidential systems founder on the same reefs, or whether their advantage over the presidential ones is indeed that they can handle divided majorities. Let the issue be phrased as follows: is there a difference, and what is the difference, between presidentialism and semi-presidentialism when it comes to split majorities, that is to say, when the majority that elects the president is not the majority that controls parliament?

There are three possible answers to the question. One is that there ultimately is no difference: in both systems a divided majority inevitably leads to conflict and gridlock. In a presidential system the conflict is between president and congress; in a semi-presidential system the conflict is between president and parliament-supported premier; but the substance is the same. The second reply is the one suggested by Vedel and Duverger, namely, that semi-presidentialism is not 'a *synthesis* of the parliamentary and presidential systems, but an *alternation* between presidential and parliamentary phases' (Duverger, 1980, p. 186). In this interpretation the French system is presidential when the president's and parliamentary majorities are consonant, and parliamentary when they are dissonant. Since I do not concur with either one of the two interpretations, I will submit shortly a third one. But first a glance at how this matter has been handled, in practice, thus far.

The first split majority came in France relatively late – between 1986 and 1988 – and the experience was relatively brief. A new period of coexistence, of *cohabitation* (as the French call it) began in June 1993, and we cannot yet tell how it will end. However, the first cohabitation went smoothly; and so far so has the second one. To be sure, no firm conclusion can be drawn on such meager evidence. And, to be sure, things went well also because Mitterrand and his 'contrary' prime ministers played their respective cards with moderation and intelligence. But the smooth working of their cohabitation cannot be simply attributed to the personality traits of the players. While hot headed leaders and compromise busters can disrupt any mechanism of power sharing, yet the French bicephalous arrangement has worked because it *can* work. While pure presidentialism is a stalemate-prone structure, semi-presidentialism proposes a gridlock-avoiding machinery. Or this is how I see it.

I was saying that I do not concur with the view of Duverger (and others) that French semi-presidentialism adds up to being an alternation between presidentialism (when the presidential and parliamentary majorities coincide) and parliamentarism (when they do not). My first objection is that the two horns of the alternative are both overstated. On the one hand a president *cum* government, that has to govern with and through another body, cannot be assimilated to the 'pure' president that governs alone, that *is* the government. Here the upgrading of the semi-presidential president is excessive (and structurally unacceptable). On the other hand, and at the other extreme, a president without majority cannot be assimilated to a standard parliamentary president. Here it is the downgrading that is excessive (and factually incorrect). A French minority president can no longer exploit his 'usurped powers' (arising from the material constitution), but never becomes a figurehead; he still is a president that stands on his own, direct legitimacy, and a president empowered by the letter of the constitution to prerogatives that parliament-elected presidents seldom if ever have.

Secondly, and foremost, I object to the 'alternation' perspective. To conceive semi-presidentialism as an alternation among two other specimens quite simply amounts to blowing apart the mixed nature of the system, and indeed asserts that here we do not have a veritable *system*. I think that this is a wholesale misunderstanding that misses the point conveyed by my notion of 'oscillation'. For alternation suggests a passage from one thing to another, while oscillation is a within-system movement. In oscillating something remains itself.

My interpretation is, then, that French semi-presidentialism has evolved into a truly *mixed system* based on a *flexible* dual authority structure, that is to say, a bicephalous executive whose 'first head' changes (oscillates) as the majority combinations change. With a unified majority the president decisively prevails over the prime minister and the constitution that applies is the material one (the conventions of the constitution). Conversely, and alternatively, with a split majority it is the prime minister supported by his own parliamentary majority that prevails, also on account of the fact that the formal constitution (what it states in writing) does support his claim to govern on his own right.

When Mitterrand yielded, in good substance, to his prime minister Chirac, he well understood that he could not win a legal fight.[4] And when, conversely, majoritarian prime ministers are nice to their president (as Balladur has been so far with Mitterrand) the underlying reasons for this pattern of behavior are, first, that the material constitution has struck roots and, second, that if their turn comes for the presidential office (an expectation that they are entitled to harbor) they too would like to be 'imperial' presidents. Let alone that both 'heads' have probably sensed that the system works precisely across the rebalancings provided by the *flexible dyarchy* that I have just outlined.

Certainly, any dual authority structure can become confrontational and thereby stalemated by an executive divided against itself. There is no assurance that this cannot and will not happen with French semi-presidentialism. Still one must recognize that in this formula the problem of divided majorities finds a solution by 'head shifting', by reinforcing the authority of whoever obtains the majority.[5] And this is a most brilliant, if unintended, piece of constitutional witchcraft.

7.2   SIMILAR AND DISSIMILAR CASES

The French Fifth Republic aside, which other countries can be classified as semi-presidential? Historically, the German Weimar constitution of 1919–1933 may rightfully be considered – in retrospect – a first configuration of a semi-presidential system. We next have two countries – Portugal and Sri Lanka – which have deliberately designed their constitutions upon the French model. A further plausible candidate for the category is Finland. And Duverger (1980) included among the semi-presidential systems also Austria, Iceland and Ireland. The Duverger list thus is: France, Weimar Republic, Portugal, Sri Lanka, Finland, Austria, Iceland and Ireland. Shugart and Carey (1993) modify it in two respects: Ireland is assigned to the parliamentary systems (I think rightly); and a new category – president-parliamentary systems – absorbs Weimar and Sri Lanka (I think messily and needlessly).

As both lists go to show, semi-presidentialism turns out to be a lumping of impossible bedfellows that defies definition.[6] Therefore, either we reduce the list to countries whose political forms truly have some common core, or we have a name for nothing, i.e., for a purely residual category.

A first pruning should immediately eliminate – I submit – Ireland, Austria and Iceland. I have already noted (*supra* 5.1) that these three countries cannot be classified as presidential purely and simply because their presidents result from popular election. On similar grounds they cannot be considered semi-presidential purely and simply because the Austrian and Icelandic presidents (not the Irish one) are strong on paper, that is, are constitutionally given powers that the living constitution relegates into inanition. With reference to the French case the 'added power' of the president must be taken into account because it is actually exercised and has in fact entered the material constitution. But when the material constitution actually deprives a president of powers that remain a dead letter of the formal constitution, then a 'dead element' surely cannot establish the nature of a political form and the class to which it belongs. Otherwise we could classify England as a monarchy – not a democracy – for no act of parliament has ever cancelled the powers that the Crown exercised, say, in the eighteenth century.

Duverger himself acknowledges that in Austria, Ireland and Iceland 'political practice is parliamentary' and that their respective presidents are 'figureheads' (1980, p. 167 and passim). What is the point, then, of assigning these countries to semi-presidentialism on a dead letter basis? Well, the point could be that under different circumstances the formal constitution still has a chance of resurrection. Indeed, dis-attended norms are not – for this reason alone – dead norms. Some legal rules remain dormant, and then are brought back to life. But some legal rules do die beyond any come-back possibility. So, do the formal constitutions in question have a chance of being resurrected? I would say no, definitely no, for Ireland and Iceland;[7] and allow a small chance, but only a small one, to Austria. In the case of Austria the acquiescent president came about, in constitutional practice, in the wake of the 'grand coalition' period, when a 90 percent parliamentary majority stood massively in the way of any possible presiden-tial interference in governmental matters. Today Austria has transformed its original two-party format in a three-party system; but this state of affairs can block any presidential activism just as effectively as the earlier one. In the case of Iceland the constitution can be amended by a simple, 51 percent majority vote, and this entails that an interfering president could be easily deprived of whatever power it tries to exercise. The Austrian lesson thus is that strong, solidary parties can always clip the wings of an activist president; and the Icelandic lesson is that overly flexible, that is, easily changeable constitutions deprive a supreme law of its supre-macy.

Remember, the examples matter because erroneous inclu-sions inevitably distort the apprehension of a specimen. Conversely put, we shall never get a handle on semi-presidentialism unless we first expel from the class its unacceptable members. But the elimination of Ireland, Ice-land and Austria leaves us with a cleaned-up list of four countries – Weimar Germany, Portugal, Sri Lanka and Finland – that begins to make sense. The reasons for the above ordering will become apparent as we proceed. And I begin with Weimar not only because it is our historical ancestor, but because the Weimar experience is as instructive as, currently, the French one.

In 1919 there was no notion of semi-presidentialism. At the time, therefore, the Weimar system was perceived as a parliamentary system counteracted by a strong presidency. The drafters of the constitution looked with awe at the French Third Republic, and their overriding concern was to impede assembly government. This was accomplished, in their design, by empowering the president i) to govern by decree, i.e., to issue, in concurrence with the Chancellor, decrees with the force of law in emergency situations (the ill reputed article 48 of the Weimar constitution), ii) to appoint and dismiss at his sole discretion the prime minister, to dismiss single cabinet ministers, and to form governments that were not subject to a parliamentary vote of confidence, iii) to dissolve parliament virtually at his discretion, iv) to refer any law approved by the *Reichstag* to popular referendum (in lieu of having veto power). As for parliament, while it was not called upon to appoint governments with a vote of confidence, it was empowered to make them fall with a vote of no-confidence (and to force the resignation of single ministers); and under normal situations it is fair to say that most of the legislative work was allocated to the *Reichstag*.

There is little question that Weimar displayed the dual authority structure that characterizes, in my account, a semi-presidential form. How close or how different was Weimar, on this score, to present-day France? The answer is complicated by the fact that the French formal constitution has evolved into a quite different material constitution. So, Weimar is compared to which? For instance, one major difference between the two formulas appears to be that the French governments need the investiture of a parliamentary vote of confidence, whereas the Weimar governments were only subject to dismissal by a vote of no-confidence. Yes and no, however. For Articles 49 and 50 of the French constitution do not speak of a parliamentary investiture of the executive and tackle the problem very much as the Weimar constitution did.

But it is unnecessary to dwell on this kind of probing, because the faltering of the Weimar Republic had little to do, in my opinion, with constitutional defects. The construction was crippled, first and foremost, by a highly fragmented and polarized party system that was nurtured, in its turn, by a 'pure' system of proportional representation (with a single national constituency). *Pace* Lijphart, more than by any other single factor Weimar was undermined by PR (a defect remedied by the French with the double ballot majority system). Another feeble point of the Weimar structure was that the president was elected by plurality, for the run-off allowed a three-man contest that impeded the emergence of a two-cornered and thus bipolar-molding race for the presidential prize.

But these are largely extra-constitutional elements. When we come to the constitution, proper, its traditional 'suspects' – the emergency powers of Article 48, and the dissolution and referendum instruments – have been over-suspected. These powers were abused, but only under circumstances that justified their abuse. Very similar provisions are found in many other constitutions and have not produced particular harms. All in all, I definitely would not say that the Weimar constitution carries the blame for the unhappy and short life of the first German republic, and especially for its downfall in Hitler's hands in 1933. Despite its imperfections, it was a cleverly and innovatively designed construction. Indeed, had Germany adopted in 1919 a parliamentary type of constitution, I believe that Weimar would have collapsed much earlier than it did – probably by 1923, when the mark was pulverized by the worst inflation ever to happen in Europe. And what did Weimar in was the 'great depression' of 1929, which hit Germany more devastatingly than any other Western country.

Turning to Portugal, this is a case that can be dealt with quickly, for its semi-presidential experience was short lived: six years between 1976–1982.[8] As regards the Portuguese constitution, its model was the French one and does not need to be rehearsed. The lesson from Lisbon is, however, that it is very unsafe to inaugurate a semi-presidential system with a minority president and, still worse, with a president without party backing. Unless semi-presidentialism obtains, at its inception, a long run of undivided majorities that consolidate the foundations, the early advent of split majorities may initially pose too much of a strain on the delicate balance of cohabitation. And this is, in essence, what happened in Portugal.

Now, Sri Lanka. The 1978 Sri Lankan constitution was also inspired by the French model (the living one), but went further in reinforcing the president's power, and this very much is the Weimar mold. Here, as in Weimar, parliament can only topple, not invest, governments. Furthermore, the Sri Lankan president, as the Weimar one, is unilaterally and discretionally entitled to outflank its legislature by submitting to referendum approval any bill rejected by parliament. Finally, and this goes beyond both France and Weimar, Sri Lanka's president is both the head of state and of the government. Legislation is thus truly initiated by the president, who also does handpick his or her ministers (very much like the American president). The question thus arises as to whether Sri Lanka is more a 'fully presidential' than a semi-presidential system. The counter-argument points out, however, that Sri Lanka does not obtain a one-person executive (as truly presidential systems require), that a parliamentary vote of no-confidence does cause the fall of the cabinet, and that a president is thereby compelled, it would appear, to select a prime minister who enjoys parliamentary support.

Clearly, we are here at the edge, somewhere between presidentialism and semi-presidentialism. But I do not feel that it is crucially important for us to decide this matter, also because it is premature to do so. Since Sri Lanka has yet to confront the acid test of a 'divided majority', it is hard to tell whether in that event a president would acquiesce or fight. He or she certainly has, in the written constitution, far more fighting force than the French president, especially on referendum grounds. Indeed the recourse to referendums has already gone as far as to extend, in 1982, the tenure of parliament for another full term of six years! On the other hand, it must also be acknowledged that this and other abuses confront a state of civil war which helps justify them. The system will have to be judged, then, if and when it will start sailing in calmer waters.

Finally, Finland, which is our oldest case since it goes all the way back to 1919. In the Finnish formula the president, who is elected indirectly, himself chairs the cabinet meetings bearing on his reserve domain, namely, 'the relation of Finland with foreign powers' (article 33). He does not attend, however, the cabinet meetings bearing on internal and administration affairs, which are chaired by the prime minister. In addition, the president does effectively choose (on the basis of the material constitution) the prime minister and does condition the coalitional composition of governments. But in all other respects Finland performs as a normal parliamentary system in which governments are voted into office and removed from office by parliament. Thus Finland well qualifies as a semi-presidential system, but for one aspect: the indirect election of its president. We shall come back to this.[9]

7.3 DEFINING SEMI-PRESIDENTIAL SYSTEMS

Having identified the cases to which the category plausibly applies, we can now revert to the unfinished business of defining semi-presidentialism. Even though we have escaped circularity, we are still confronted with the difficulty of pinning down a two-headed configuration that also displays a significant variance across its cases. How far can we go – in establishing defining characteristics – in firming up who has power over whom, in what manner and/or circumstances, and when does a dual authority cease to be dual? If we try to be overly precise, we easily end up with a class with just one case. If, on the other hand, we seek refuge in overly loose formulations, then the primary purpose of defining – the drawing of borders – is defeated. I shall try to steer a somewhat discursive middle course between overdefining and underdefining. Bearing the foregoing provisos in mind I stipulate that a political system is semi-presidential if the following properties or characteristics jointly apply:

i)   The head of state (president) is elected by popular vote – either directly or indirectly – for a fixed term of office.

ii) The head of state shares the executive power with a prime minister, thus entering a dual authority structure whose three defining criteria are:

iii) The president is independent from parliament, but is not entitled to govern alone or directly and therefore his will must be conveyed and processed via his government.

iv) Conversely, the prime minister and his cabinet are president-independent in that they are parliament-dependent: they are subject to either parliamentary confidence or no-confidence (or both), and in either case need the support of a parliamentary majority.

v)   The dual authority structure of semi-presidentialism allows for different balances and also for shifting prevalences of power within the executive, under the strict condition that the 'autonomy potential' of each component unit of the executive does subsist.

Clearly, a mixed form is never as simple as a pure form. That the definition of semi-presidentialism had to be less tidy and more complicated than the one of presidentialism (*supra* 5.1) was in the cards and cannot surprise us. The immediate question is: how does my definition compare with other ones? Shugart and Carey deserve the credit of having made the first serious and systematic attempt at defining political forms, and their proposal for semi-presidentialism rejects the label and breaks the specimen into two regime types: i) premier-presidential and ii) president-parliamentary (1992, pp. 18–27 and passim). The first is characterized by the primacy of the premier over the president, the second by the primacy of the president.

Under this distinction, however, the French system (and prototype) breaks in two, for it characteristically switches this 'primacy' from president to premier, and vice versa.[10] And I cannot accept their distinction on other grounds as well. My second misgiving is that the Shugart–Carey criteria still admit Austria and Iceland in the premier-presidential category (and thus, in substance, into semi-presidentialism); and this attests, it seems to me, to a serious lack of discriminating power. My third misgiving is that their president-parliamentary category turns out to be an almost empty class, a container in desperate want of content.[11] And here my point is that there is no point in trying to extract a category from quicksand. So, does their dumping of 'semi-presidentialism' and the distinction thus resulting really sustain discernible and discernibly important differences? I think not.

Reverting to my definition, two explications are in order. As regards the first criterion let me recall that in the case of pure presidentialism the formulation was that the president results from 'direct or direct-like popular elections', whereas in the case of semi-presidentialism I say that the president is elected 'either directly or indirectly' by popular vote. The rewording is not casual, and I am not engaging in hair splitting. Under the first formulation (until the 1994 election) the Finnish president cannot be counted as a popularly elected president, whereas under the second formulation he can. Of course, the issue is not Finland. The issue is how stringent we want the criterion to be. The difference between 'direct-like' (or quasi-direct) and 'indirect' is that the second formulation permits the understanding that a head of state that is *not* elected by parliament qualifies as a 'true president' (a presidential president) also when his election is a two-step election. In the latter case the popular vote elects an *ad hoc* electoral college, which in turn freely chooses and thus truly elects the president.[12] One may wonder why I make such a fuss of this. Why not simply let Finland exit from semi-presidentialism and describe its polity as a parliamentary system *cum* strong president? Well, my reason is that I harbor a future-oriented worry: video-politics and video-power, that is to say, how television and the mass media age are radically affecting politics and, in the case at hand, the presidential selection process.[13]

To begin with, it is clearly the case that video-politics facilitates the election of improvised and, indeed, flash 'outsiders'. *Prima facie* this may appear to be a good thing. But these outsider-presidents are presidents without troops. Take Fujimori in Peru and Collor in Brazil, and forget whether they are or have been capable presidents: the point remains that their presidency has or had no partisan support. Fujimori cannot even reclaim himself to a party; and while Collor improvised a party as he campaigned for his election, his party made less than 10 percent of the vote thus leaving him 40 percent short of even a nominal majority. To be sure, two cases do not establish a trend. But the symptoms and the seeds are there. In Peru the antagonist of Fujimori was another outsider, the novelist Vargas Llosa; and in the United States had not Ross Perot made a couple of colossal mistakes (as the one of withdrawing-reentering at mid-race) he was coming very close, in 1992, to being elected president.

A second development – and a high-risk one – is that video-politics turns a presidential election into a very chancy event. The American president has increasingly been the winner of a video-match eminently decided by looks and 'sound bytes' of 10 seconds (their average in 1988). Video-elections are supposed to bring about transparence, true 'visible politics'. Alas, no. What we are actually given, under the guise of visibility, is largely a display of petty appearances that leaves the issues in greater darkness than ever. The long and short of my brief thus is that the popular, direct election of presidents provides no safeguards and no buffers against a disastrous election (misselection) of the all-decider – and that this will be ever more the case. More than ever before videopolitics promises to put in office improvised dilettantes and/or poll-monitored robots (whose true faces are never unveiled) stuck with populist campaign promises.

On these considerations why deny equal legitimacy to a president-making process that allows for the close and competent scrutiny that direct elections under video monitoring surely do not allow? Finland owes a great deal to having been able to choose 'right presidents', for not only Finland had to confront the menace – a very real one – of the Soviet Union, but also displayed a highly infelicitous party system of 'polarized pluralism'. But the issue, I was saying, is not about Finland per se. The issue is whether we accept a Finnish 1919–94 'model' as a form of semi-presidentialism. I propose that we do, perhaps especially for the benefit of the Eastern European and of the formerly Soviet countries.

My second explication with regard to the definition of semi-presidentialism is simply and briefly this: that my last three criteria basically address the problem of sorting out a dual authority structure, on the assumption that this is *the* distinctive feature of the specimen. Other characteristics, important as they may be, run across other political forms as well. For instance, 'the power to dissolve parliament, or legislative powers' (Shugart and Carey, 1992, p. 24) are attributes that must either be detailed far more specifically, or that have, as stated, no discriminating value. A British prime minister can be said to have, in some sense or other, 'legislative powers' just as much as any president, both of the pure and impure varieties; and the power to dissolve parliament is given, in some form or other, to almost all parliamentary heads of state. Whereas the primary purpose of *defining characteristics* is to establish the cut-off points between something and what we perceive to be something else (Sartori, 1984b, pp. 28–34).

7.4 WHICH IS BEST?

In the conclusion of the First Part I answered the 'which is best' question by indicating a somewhat generalized preference, among electoral systems, for some form of double ballot. But as regards 'whole systems' – the theme of Part Two – it would be foolhardy, I believe, to be as bold. For that political form is best that applies best. A conclusion that also implies that there is no getting away from context.

Latin Americans are advised to adopt parliamentarism, but the French have dismissed it with relish. Many Englishmen are frustrated by their two-party straitjacket, but most Italians think that the English system is great. We are generally justified in criticizing the polity under which we live, but often wrong in assessing its alternative and its hoped for benefits. I believe that the case *against* the two extremes, pure presidentialism and pure parliamentarism, is a strong one. By the same token I believe that the positive case *for* 'mixed systems' is equally strong. However, to argue that mixed systems are better than pure ones, is not to argue that among the mixed forms semi-presidentialism is the best one. This is an ulterior step that I am not prepared to take unqualifiedly.

Let me start with the assertion that semi-presidentialism is better than presidentialism. This has in fact been my thesis – especially on the ground that the former system can cope with split majorities far better than the latter. I also hold that countries that intend to leave presidentialism are well advised to opt for semi-presidentialism on grounds of prudence – on account of the fact that for a presidential country a leap to parliamentarism is a leap into the utterly diverse and unknown, whereas a switch to semi-presidentialism still allows that country to perform in the ambit of what it knows, of the experience and expertise that it has.

Does the same advice hold – symmetrically and from the other end of the spectrum – for the countries that wish to abandon their parliamentarism? Should they too contemplate – as the alternative that best suits them – semi-parliamentarism (premiership systems) rather than semi-presidentialism? In theory it might look that way, but in practice it does not. For here the problem is that the implantation of premiership systems largely defies constitutional engineering (*supra* 6.3). The English or German-type of muzzled parliamentarism perform as they are intended to perform only under a set of favorable conditions. If the English system ceased to be a twoparty system (in which third parties have never managed, thus far, to break single-party governance), or if the German polity became more fragmented and more polarized than it has been thus far, both 'models' would vanish into thin air. And this implies that a country that seeks for itself a semi-parliamentary solution embarks on a very hazardous journey, for too many assumptions must hold for this transplant to succeed.

To belabor the point, the parliamentary countries that are the most unhappy with their experience are likely to be the least-working parliamentary democracies and most probably the assembly-driven ones. It should be further assumed that the countries in question display a fragmented party system of the type that I call 'extreme pluralism'. And if this is the case, we are also probably dealing with PR countries that have long indulged themselves with 'proportional politics'. But from this start the incremental going from pure parliamentarism to premiership parliamentarism is an uphill fight that is all too easily lost. From this point of departure the easiest path is not the one of gradually moving into semi-parliamentarism, but the one of radically switching to semi-presidentialism. This is not only attested by the French experience, but also sustained by the argument that semi-presidentialism is far more amenable to constitutional engineering than premiership systems.[14]

Note, however, that my argument is not – in the context of parliamentarism – that semi-presidentialism 'is best' but, rather, that it is 'more applicable'. It is on two different grounds and by two different routes, then, that I end up with generally recommending – to the change advocates – semi-presidentialism. And I further wish to underscore that this recommendation is not a strong one. Semi-presidentialism does leave us with unsettled problems.[15] Nor do I deny that semi-presidentialism is a somewhat fragile system. The split majority problem still haunts – if to a far lesser degree than in pure presidentialism – the semi-presidential experience. Can we do better and find a more solid and efficient mixed system? This is the question that I plan to explore in Part Three.

NOTES

1. Cf. *contra* Shugart and Carey (1993, p. 22 and passim) who replace 'semi-presidentialism' on the argument that 'semi' suggests 'a regime type that is located midway along some continuum'. But *semi* is the Latin for 'half', and – as any dictionary would show for hundreds of expressions – does not assume any continuum because it precedes continuum-mania by well over two thousand years.
2. Duverger, 1980, p. 171. In short, and apart from the exceptional powers granted in article 16, the constitution empowers the president to have recourse (though not unilaterally) to

referendums, to dissolve parliament, and somewhat gives him a reserve domain in matters of defense and of foreign politics. The president can also effectively block action by his *pouvoir d'empecher*, either by veto or by refusing to sign decrees.

3. On January 31, 1964, De Gaulle proclaimed 'that the indivisible authority of the state is entrusted completely to the president by the people who elected him' and that 'the supreme domain is his alone'. Nothing of this is in the Debré constitution; but De Gaulle's successors, all the way up to Mitterrand, have been happy to oblige.

4. To exemplify, the more patent 'usurpation' of presidential powers has occurred with referendums, that De Gaulle and his successors have decided on their own whereas the constitution requires, for referendums (article 11), joint action with the cabinet or with the two chambers. This practice went unopposed; but if a 'minority Mitterrand' initiated a referendum, he could or indeed would be blocked. Likewise, constitutionally the president is not empowered to dismiss the prime minister; he did so cavalierly in the past; but with a split majority he is unlikely to try.

5. If this interpretation is correct, it takes care, I submit, of Linz's objection to semi-presidentialism (1990, p. 63) that 'No democratic principle exists to resolve disputes between the executive and the legislature about which of the two actually represents the will of the people'.

6. The reason for this is, it appears, that interpreters never quite make up their mind as to whether their referent is the formal constitution, the material constitution, and/or the go-between among the two. The interplay of these elements (as I understand it) comes out in my analysis of the French case, and will be detailed further as we proceed.

7. The Irish constitution does not attribute any particular power to its president; so in this case there is nothing to resurrect. And in Iceland the atrophy of the presidential office has reached its point of no return with the practice of automatically renewing the term of office of the president when no candidate opposes him or her.

8. The 1982 Portuguese constitution eliminates the presidential power to dismiss cabinets or ministers (unless democratic institutions are threatened, article 198) and all his legislative powers; and restricts his power to dissolve parliament as well as his pocket veto on legislation. By and large, the Portuguese

president is thus left, from 1982 onward, with the normal powers of normal parliamentary presidents.

9. In December 1993 also Russia has entered the category of semi-presidential systems with a constitution hastily adopted by referendum. My provisional understanding (from indirect sources) of the Yeltsin constitution is that it is derived from the French model with a confrontational twist, however, that is shunned by the Fifth Republic. To wit, the President appoints the prime minister and its deputy; but if the Duma rejects their nomination for three times, then the President may dissolve the lower house and call for new elections. And the same applies to a no confidence vote in the government expressed twice. What I read between the lines of these provisions is that the President must win anyhow. Be that as it may, within the range of variation of semi-presidentialisms, Yeltsin's constitution clearly empowers a dominant president and Russia comes to represent the strong extreme of a continuum along which Finland represents the feeble extreme.

10. And then, why is France assigned to the premier-presidential type? For most of the time, and on the basis of the material constitution, the Fifth Republic ought to be assigned to the president-parliamentary type.

11. To wit, the president-parliamentary cases are Ecuador, Germany (Weimar), Korea, Peru, Sri Lanka (see their pp. 40–41). But for Germany, all the other cases are as evanescent as they can be. South Korean presidentialism was only a flash transition (1988–90); Ecuador is one of the most unstable and crisis ridden regimes in the world; Sri Lanka is, we have seen, a highly debatable case; and Peru is, at the time of this writing, in constitutional remaking. As for Weimar I cannot find any valid reason for its inclusion in the category. If it is their criterion 2 ('the president appoints and dismisses cabinet ministers'), then the Weimar president did not handpick the cabinet members; and if it is their criterion 3 ('cabinet ministers are subject to parliamentary confidence'), this is inaccurate.

12. That in Finland the election of the electoral college was in fact party controlled and abided by party lines is immaterial to the point. The indirectness would be the same without party control, though the chances of obtaining strongly minoritarian presidents would increase. Shugart and Carey (1992, p. 221) argue that the party-centered presidential election without pledged votes in Finland has not been 'much different from

election in parliament'. But a comparison between Finland and Italy – two countries with very similar party systems – attests to very important differences. And then Shugart and Carey overlook the legitimacy difference.

13. The point is developed and placed in context *infra* 8.3.

14. It should be well understood that throughout this work 'constitutional engineering' is a shorthand that includes the electoral system, even though electoral systems are generally determined by ordinary legislation (though not always; not in Austria, for example). This is so on substantive grounds, because every political form hinges on its electoral arrangements just as much as on its architectural (and more properly constitutional) ones.

15. As we shall see in Part Three, chaps. 9 and 10, it does not provide, for instance, a satisfactory solution to the problem of 'governing by legislating'.

Part Three
Issues and Proposals

8 The Difficulty of Politics

8.1 DEMOCRATIC PRIMITIVISM AND NEGATIVISM

If we pause to think about it, managing politics was a far easier, indeed an immensely easier matter, say, a century ago. The increasing difficulty of politics results from many reasons. Intellectually it goes back to the late sixties, when the campus revolution brought to the fore a new democratic primitivism. However, the seeds of difficult politics are also technological and have a lot to do with video-democracy. And, in the interim, we are confronted with degenerative processes, especially an escalation of political corruption that corrupts politics itself.

It is an already discovered truth that making things appear simpler than they are actually complicates them. As Mencken once said, 'For every human problem there is a solution that is simple, neat and wrong'. And during the sixties a generation came of age that did believe that it had simple and neat solutions for just about everything. The generation of the campus revolution told itself that 'real democracy' simply consisted of empowering more and more people with more and more power. Neat — but wrong. Democracy cannot simply be power of the people, because this is a shorthand for the full expression 'power of the people *over* the people'. Power is a relation, and to have power implies that somebody controls (in some manner or extent) somebody else. Furthermore real power is a power that is exercised. So, how can a whole people — tens or even hundreds of millions of people — exercise power over themselves? There is no neat answer to that.

In like manner the cultural revolution (the Western one, to be sure) of the sixties developed the belief that real democracy had to be 'full democracy' — democracy everywhere — and this implied that political democracy needed the complement of economic democracy. Easy? It was made to appear easy because the argument simply required (in its non-marxist variety) the extending to the plant, or to the offices of the post-industrial society, of the mechanisms of self-government of political democracy. The complication that passed unnoticed and that remains unaddressed was that economic democracy still had to be 'economic', that it had to deal with economics. And there surely is no easy answer to how democratic decision-making squares with costs, productivity, profits, and with swimming in world-wide competitive markets.

As the high hopes of the rebels of the sixties foundered on the reefs of reality, their leftover was, deep down, a deep dislike of the world that had survived their attack. While the simplistic solutions devised by the *imagination au pouvoir* have dissolved themselves by themselves, their legacy remains very much with us under the form of 'simplistic negativism'. There is so much that always goes wrong in the real world that one is never mistaken in choosing the path of 'criticism'. Fine. But is criticism an end in itself? For the negativist, yes. The negativist never asks: What is the purpose? Where does my attack lead or go? Nor does he ask: What are the alternatives? The suspicion that the alternatives might be worse, or that there are no available alternatives, seldom if ever crosses his mind.

The net result of 'simplism' – the combination of infantile democracy and simplistic negativism – thus is that the old watch of politics receives a lot of clubbing, but no sound advice on how it could be repaired and/or changed for the better. Indeed, the more we break it, the less we are capable of fixing it. By the same token we have invested all our ingenuity in expanding 'horizontal democracy' and have not only neglected but actually debunked, in the process, 'vertical democracy'. Which is to say that for many decades we have seemingly forgotten, and certainly overlooked, that in the end democracy is, and cannot avoid being, a *system of government*. And by neglecting the governing function we worsen or even imperil its functioning.

8.2 CORRUPTION AND THE REJECTION OF POLITICS

Politicians are popular in heroic times, but are seldom popular in times of routine, when the politics of democracy becomes an ordinary, day by day, muddling through. Invectives against politicians abound in the so-called anti-parliamentary literature of the late nineteenth century, and recur ever since. Thus *disencanto*, a disenchantment and disillusion with politics, is nothing new. Yet when Lipset and Schneider (1983) reported about the 'confidence gap' between citizens and their elected representatives, they were detecting an unprecedented trend. And in a number of countries disillusion and distrust have currently swelled into a crescendo of frustration, anger and, in the end, of outright rejection of politics. In the end, then, we are confronted with a surge of anti-politics, with what we might call the *politics of anti-politics*.

How did it come to that? There are several explanations for this rejection. One of them is the negativism that we have just reviewed.[1] Television also concurs. A third factor probably is the dissolution of the cement of ideology. But the single best explanation for today's anger lies, I believe, in political corruption. Politics has never been, and will probably never be, immaculate; and political corruption is by no means a newcomer. But greed and corruption have recently reached unprecedented heights. Political corruption has indeed reached the point at which it corrupts politics.

Let me immediately qualify the above. When I say that corruption corrupts politics I intend that it corrupts 'democratic politics'. For in other contexts making money out of politics may not be, nor be perceived as, corruption. Corruption becomes corruption only when political entities reach the stage of structural differentiation that provides – in the wording of Max Weber – for a 'rational-legal' bureaucracy. In particular, corruption becomes corruption only when a service becomes a 'public service' (rendered by elected officials and/or by civil servants on the state's payroll) that entitles citizens to receive it free of charge. Africa, much of the

Middle East and of Asia are generally spoken of as areas of total corruption. But this is an overly sweeping generalization that ill-applies to countries in which political office still is an appendage of wealth and lineage, and where it is normal for politics to be a source of, and means to, riches. However, when 'corruption' properly applies, then it has two sides. On the one side we have politicians and civil servants that are bribed, that are bought into doing or not doing things and, on the other side, we have politicians that extort money for their political career and that, in the process, also steal it for themselves.

Here, and once again, we must be careful in generalizing. Corruption is certainly rampant in much of Latin America. In 1993 Brazil's President, Collor, and also Perez, the President of Venezuela, have been forced out of office on corruption charges. Corruption is also a serious problem in Argentina and in many other Latin American countries. In Europe, Italy's party system has been literally wiped out, again in 1993, by corruption related scandals; and Japan too has been deeply wounded in the last few years by political money scandals. Let it be added that also Communist regimes have been deeply corrupt regimes, and that the demise of communism has, if anything, intensified the corruption. However, and clearly, there are countries that have resisted corruption far better than others. My generalizing taps on a trend; and a very uneven one at that. Yet the dirty politics of dirty money has been by and large on the increase for quite some time. And there are three reasons for that.

The first reason is the loss of ethics and, specifically, of the ethics of 'public service'. A second, formidable reason is that there simply is too much money around. And a third, related reason is that the cost of politics has become excessive and largely out of control.[2] The bottom line is this: that as ethical restraints fade, temptations grow also because they knock at our doors all the time and in staggering amounts. Drug money is just one example among many. Many prices are and have to be controlled (medicine prices, utility prices, etc.); and a near-infinite amount of items require permits, regulation, inspection. The occasions for bribery and extortion are, by the same token, just as infinite. In part, this dirty money is 'necessary money' for meeting the cost of getting oneself elected; but in part it also enters the pockets of the permit-givers.

How can the corruption of politics be counteracted? Certainly the cost of politics can and must be reduced. Certainly electoral expenses can and must be capped.[3] And the more the state can be made to withdraw from extra-political areas, the lesser the occasions and temptations of political corruption. Also, penalties must be stiffened, truly effective controls must be imposed. All of this is easy to propose and to spell out. But corruption and greed are self-sustaining. A shock was needed – and fortunately that shock is coming. The lid on political corruption is now being blown up. Today corruption is exposed and highly resented. Indeed, the outcry of the day is an outcry about and against political corruption.

There is no doubt in my mind that democracies must clean up their act, and that the 'cleaning of politics' is a major priority of our time. But as this cleaning occurs, politics becomes a greater hurdle race than ever. If politicians are generally (though not always deservedly) distrusted,[4] and if parties as such fall in disrepute,[5] then we have a game with missing pieces. Note that disenchantment and disillusion may also lead to apathy, to a withdrawal from politics, to what was called, in the fifties, 'depoliticization'. But the rejection of politics that is swelling today is not at all passive, but active, participant and vindictive. And while the apathetic citizen made politics too easy, the actively vindictive citizen may make it too difficult.

Let me say again – for I do not wish to be misunderstood – that the broom of anti-politics is a most necessary broom. On balance, its excesses outweigh its drawbacks. Yet, as the dirty water of corruption is thrown overboard the baby must be saved. The distaste of parties and the disrepute of politicians inevitably reflect themselves on the institutions in which they are housed. And if representative institutions themselves are generally perceived as inadequate instruments of democracy, then the saving of the baby becomes quite a task.

8.3   VIDEO-POLITICS AND VIDEO-DEMOCRACY

Simplistic negativism and the distrust of politics may, and hopefully will, pass. Instead the media revolution and, in its wake, video-politics and video-democracy are with us for good. But, first, the media revolution itself. For the power of the video extends far beyond the sphere of politics. Indeed, television is in the process of reshaping our very way of being.

Homo sapiens is, or has developed himself into becoming, a reading animal capable of abstraction, whose understanding (intelligence, *intelligere*) goes far beyond his seeing, and actually is quite unrelated to what he sees. But *homo sapiens* is in the process of being displaced and replaced by *homo videns*, a television-made animal whose mind is no longer shaped by concepts, by abstract mental constructs, but by images. *Homo videns* just 'sees' (*videre* is the Latin for the verb 'to see'), and its horizon is confined to the images that he or she is given to see. Thus while *homo sapiens* is entitled to say, in all innocence, 'I see' to mean 'I understand', *homo videns* sees unassisted by understanding. For much of what he is shown has little significance, and what is significant is, at best, poorly explained.[6]

Reverting to my theme, video-politics has already entered my argument tangentially with reference to how it affects the choosing of presidents (*supra* 7.3); but, needless to say, it equally affects the choosing of any and all elected officials. Furthermore, video-politics deeply affects the choices, i.e., the decisions that politicians make. For politicians react more and more not to events in themselves, but to media-events, that is to say, to what is made video-visible and even to media-initiated (and largely media fabricated) events.[7] And, of course, video-politics changes the citizen itself, for the video-citizen that 'sees politics' in images is an entirely new protagonist in, or of the political process.

The balance sheet of the television age displays, like all balance sheets, assets and liabilities. Video-politics is very good at 'exposing' wrongs and wrongdoings (or non-doings). It does also very well in heating and mobilizing audiences into fighting for worthy (but also unworthy) causes. For instance, it does marvels in denouncing political corruption and all kinds of abuses. Television also receives credit for extending more information to more people. But here I start having doubts; here the assets of video-politics give way to its liabilities. Information is not the sheer notifying of the 'news' (what is new) of the day; for an informed public is supposed to be able to pass an informed judgment. Is that the case? I think not. The television-fed public is, by all counts, a highly disinformed and ill-informed public. Television does reach larger audiences; but its visual messages, its newscasting, provide the semblance, not the substance of information. More people are fed with less, and with greater shallowness. At the same time the public is fed with affect-based information, with images that stir compassion or anger, but that 'warm up' problems far beyond our capability of solving them. And I see no gain in that.

The upshot is this: that the priorities of television are the scoop, the shoot (a good image), and the ratings (the largest possible audience). And these are bound to be wrong priorities, priorities that are both overblown and wrongly ordered. The politician generally hunts for votes once very four years. Television makes its own vote count every day. Perforce, then, the medium is frivolous, irresponsible and populistic. We can have, of course, elite video-politics besides mass video-politics. But elite television is watched by the few; whereas mass television carries the many, the money and, in the process, also the votes. When it comes to the news hour (or half-hour) the astute television producer tells the viewer: we let you (people like you) speak for themselves, and/or it is up to you, the people as a whole, to tell us what you feel and like. The screen is thus filled with 'casual interviews' in which a well doctored mix of faces is given five seconds of talking glory, or otherwise displays an anchor-person who reverentially reports that the polls establish this and that.

Much of both is farce and swindle. The casual interviewee does not constitute a sample of anything, does not 'represent' (statistically) anything, and in serious matters this genre eminently works as an amplifier and multiplier of stupidities. Nor do polls reveal the 'voice of the people'; rather, they reveal the voice *of* the media *in* the people – they largely are a *reflection effect* of the media. How do the people know, for instance, who is to be believed about something? They don't – aside from responding to what they listen to. And since the amount of selective omission (and also distortion) that goes into the visual message is staggering, it turns out, in the end, that the people of the media age truly are 'media fabricated' people.

But the above opens up arguments that cannot be pursued here.[8] For my brief only is to show how difficult politics has become. Let my winding up simply be, then, that video-politics produces increasing affect-mobilized participation under conditions of decreasing and impoverished information. And if this is the case, surely 'doing politics' (good politics) is in trouble. Let us at least see to it that the house of politics is kept in order and that democracy as a system of government is helped by helpful structures – the task to which I now return.

NOTES

1. To be sure, 'criticism at all cost' and the politics of anti-politics overlap and reinforce each other. However, one is an intellectual negation, and the other a grass-roots reaction.
2. In the respective more recent elections, in Japan the cost of an LDP seat averaged more than 7 million U.S. dollars; in the U.S.A. the bill for a Senate seat in California reached 10 million dollars (the country average was 4 million) and the biennial spending on congressional elections is around $500 million; and in Italy the cost of the 1992 election has been estimated in the order of 1.500 billion lire (about 900 million dollars).
3. Absurdly, the U.S. Supreme Court has ruled that capping the amounts that candidates may spend is an unconstitutional infringement of 'free speech' rights. But this overstretching of the concept of free speech remains, to date, an isolated case.
4. A typical manifestation of this distrust is, in the United States, the term limit for elected office (generally, two or three mandates) already approved by referendum in several states.

5. Tellingly, new-born parties tend to call themselves something else: movements, alliances, leagues, *rassemblements*. This is quite different, note, from the understandable rejection of the word party in the former communist countries.
6. The counterargument is that *homo sapiens* and *homo videns* blend with one another. This may still be the case for the time being. But we definitely are in transit from one prevalence to another prevalence; and to perceive this as a blending is to blind ourselves to the seriousness of the problem.
7. I am not the first to note that American foreign policy decisions are being shaped and dictated, more and more, by video displays. President Reagan probably fell into the Iran-gate mess because the weeping images of the parents of kidnapped hostages were all over the screen. And, in 1993, why intervene, e.g., in Somalia rather than in Sudan and, for that matter, in several equally needy African countries? In these and numberless other instances policies go where television goes.
8. They are pursued and amplified in Sartori 1989, and Sartori 1992 (ch. 15, pp. 303–15).

9 Alternating Presidentialism: A Proposal

9.1 FROM ONE ENGINE TO TWO

Presidentialism and parliamentarism are single-engine mechanisms. In the first system the engine is the president, in the second the engine is parliament. And far more often than not the presidential engine falters in its downward parliamentary crossings, while the parliamentary engine disarrays, in its upward ascent, the governing function. Semi-presidentialism is, instead, a double-engine system. However, since its two engines operate simultaneously, what if they start pulling in opposite directions and work against one another? While the French system is able to handle divided government, still the risk of having two counter-pulling engines cannot be ruled out.

The foregoing considerations prompt me to seek a twin-motor system whose engines are not simultaneous but ignited in succession: the system that can either be called *alternating presidentialism*, or *intermittent presidentialism*.[1] The basic idea is to have a parliamentary system goaded or otherwise punished by a presidential displacement and replacement. So long as the parliamentary system works, it is allowed to endure. But if it fails to meet given standards, then the parliamentary engine is switched off and a presidential engine supplants it. The basic idea is thus to have – during the course of each legislature – a carrot that rewards performance and a stick that sanctions misconduct.

It should be understood from the outset that while the alternating presidentialism proposal assumes as its baseline a parliamentary system, this does not entail that its applicability is restricted to existing parliamentary polities. Suppose that we have an impossible presidential system that cannot be made to work by incremental improvement. In such event it can be turned into a parliamentary system that also contemplates, within its mechanisms, its own correction.

Latin American presidential systems that are searching for an alternative solution have, in my opinion, two options. One is French-type semi-presidentialism – a solution that would improve upon American-type presidentialism and yet remains an insufficient remedy for countries like Brazil and, more generally, for any polity characterized by parliamentary atomization and fluid or excessive multipartism. The other option is not, however, standard parliamentarism (*supra* 6.5), but a self-redressing one. It equally seems to me (on very different grounds, to be sure) that the formula of alternating presidentialism would suit Mexico – along its long march away from over-concentrated power – far better than a semi-presidential formula.[2] And it specially strikes me that the largely unworkable constitutions hastily concocted in many formerly communist countries have nothing to lose and would have much to gain by experimenting with a segment of parliamentarism corrected and/or counteracted by a subsequent segment of presidentialism.

Resuming my thread, the question is: How can constitutional mechanisms promote good government and obstruct bad government? Good government can be simply defined, for the purpose at hand, as governments that are enabled to perform and encouraged to perform responsibly. *Per contra*, bad government consists of governments that are unstable, incompetent, inefficient and/or powerless. Lest the tone be pitched too high, the above simply means that governments should not be shot down just because MP's like to become cabinet ministers; that cabinets should not be composed of factional bosses in utter disrespect of capabilities and competence; and that it makes no sense to repair impotent governments with other impotent governments, that is, with the sheer repetition of the same patchwork: garbage in, garbage out, and then garbage in again.

9.2   STRONG-INTERMITTENT PRESIDENCY

So, how can governments be helped to perform and encouraged to perform responsibly? The formula that I have in mind – alternating presidentialism – pursues this end in three ways, that is to say, via three structural arrangements.

First, every newly elected parliament is allowed to vote in office one government if the legislature lasts four years, and two governments if its duration is five years. This means that under its first, or two first governments, the political system will perform under the normal rules of normal parliamentarism.

Second, if and when the government(s) allocated to the parliamentary method fail, then a 'strong' presidential mechanism takes over for the remaining duration of the legislature. This entails that the president also heads the government, that he or she appoints and dismisses discretionally the cabinet members, and that the government is neither subject to a vote of confidence nor dismissable by a parliamentary vote of non-confidence. Conversely, and by the same token, the role of parliament is now drastically reduced to a control role.

Third, the president is indirectly or directly elected by an absolute majority of the popular vote, its tenure coincides with the duration of parliament (four or five years), and can be reelected without term limit. It should be well understood that during the parliamentary period the president remains a normal parliamentary president (as, say, in Austria); that his direct and independent legitimacy is, at the outset, a 'reserve' legitimacy; and that what could also happen is that the presidential alternation is not triggered. But if this is so, it probably means that the deterrent has been effective, that its purpose was achieved.

These are the broad strokes. Now the details. A first general point is that under the alternating presidentialism arrangement the hand of the initial parliamentary-based government(s) would be significantly strengthened, for all the parties in the play well understand that a government that falls is also a parliament that downsizes itself. At the same time, and concurrently, the members of parliament can no longer perceive the yearly massacre of governments as their yearly chance of grabbing a cabinet position for themselves. With a four-year legislature the 'armchair hunting' begins and ends with the first government; with a five-year legislature, chair hunters have only one shot to go – and the game is too short to be worth playing. Under these two considerations it can be reasonably expected, then, that the parliamentary-based government(s) would not only last longer, but also that their governing would be more effective and assertive than otherwise.

This element of my proposal has been subjected to two divergent criticisms. The conjecture of some critics has been that an anti-presidential alliance would see to it that the presidential engine is never ignited. The conjecture of other critics has been, instead, that a presidentialist conspiracy would activate the presidential alternative with undue haste. Since the two scenarios cancel each other out, they comfort my expectation that from one-third to one-half of the legislature's time will either be parliamentary or presidential. For I do not see how a do-nothing government could be kept alive for four years when a do-something alternative knocks at its door. On the other hand, parliaments are only too happy to place on somebody else's lap the unpopular measures that they hate to underwrite; and on this score the passing of the buck to a president-in-waiting comes, or may come, as a welcome relief. As for the contrary conjecture, I do not see any 'presidentialist conspiracy' arising from nowhere, that is, without rewards or benefits coming to the conspirators.

Turning to the second feature of alternating presidentialism, the crucial question is: How 'strong' should the presidentialist interregnum be? The key to the answer is that we are in fact dealing with an *interregnum*. Presidential systems cannot contemplate intermittent presidents, and therefore cannot afford (without too much risk) overly powerful presidents. But an intermittent president whose term ends with the fixed end of each legislature, that can never reinstate himself as a presidentialist president at the outset of any legislature, and whose likely cycle of real power runs from two to three years, drastically reduces the risk factor. My formula thus allows for strong presidents. But exactly how strong?

In standard presidential systems presidents are generally strong in the executive domain – they *are* in control of their government and of the surrounding spoils – and generally weak in the legislative arena, in their parliamentary outreach. The problem thus is one of legislative power (and will be examined in the next chapter). Instead the executive power of an alternating president poses no problem; when in charge, he or she performs just like a pure president. Since the government is not subject to parliamentary conditionings, he or she does have a free pick in choosing and dismissing cabinet members. Remember, however, that the alternating president may be tempted to promote and accelerate his or her coming to power. Therefore the president must not be permitted to reward with a portfolio the MP's that have 'conspired' in his or her favor. Alternating presidentialism requires, then, a strict incompatibility between parliamentary and ministerial office.[3] An incompatibility which is not only a necessary precaution but also – in my judgment – a good thing per se, for it is good to have, periodically, governments of outsiders (and, better still, governments of experts) competing with the governments of politicians.

The third element of alternating presidentialism is that president and parliament must be elected at the same time and must also terminate together. This is a most crucial condition, for it firmly sets intervals, intermittent time limits, to the power of the presidency. It is equally important, on the other hand, not to limit the president's reelection, for a president that does well must be rewarded. And the discontinuous nature of his full power removes the reasons that otherwise justify term limits. Finally, the president must be elected by an absolute majority, preferably via the double ballot method. And I further suggest that the whole machinery would work more smoothly if also the parliamentary election was double-ballot based. In this manner we obtain a 'presidentialization' of electoral behavior conducive to bipolar aggregations which help, in turn, the parliamentary performance of the system. Even though the presidential prize is not as decisive, with alternating presidentialism, as it is with the French Fifth Republic, the analogies are strong enough to justify the same electoral arrangements across the board.

9.3   THE BEST OF TWO WORLDS?

As the scheme is appraised in its entirety, some further merits become apparent. To begin with, in my proposal there is no need for early elections and for having recourse to the dissolution of parliament. I take this to be a merit on two counts: because frequent elections overheat politics and bring about an excess of irresponsible electoral politics; and because there is no assurance that new elections will produce different parliaments and thus provide a solution for the problems that prompted that early call. Italy has had, between 1968 and 1987, a series of five early elections that left matters exactly where they were. And the Weimar Republic was helped in its collapse by a series of four consecutive dissolutions of the *Reichstag* between 1930 and 1933 that only made things worse. So, early dissolutions are often useless and at times counter-productive. In their stead the solution of changing – at some midpoint of a legislature – engine and driver is costless and surely of consequence.

A parallel merit of alternating presidentialism is that it puts a lid on the budget-busting spending spree that characteristi-cally precedes elections as long as incumbents are thus helped to 'buy' their reelection. Instead, with alternating presidenti-alism when election time comes parliament is likely to be under ice and thus unable to request or authorize any budget spending. As for the president, my sense is that its most rewarding electoral tactic is to run as a countervailing player, as a 'corrector' of parliamentary feeblenesses and largesses.

But why should our intermittent president behave as my argument expects? Well, because this is the role expectation built into the system, and because his or her gratifications and rewards are all geared to a performance of effectiveness. Of course, and once again, the caveat is that structures cannot substitute persons. The wrong person will do badly even when the structure is right. But wrong structures waste the right person. Assume that our president has been ill-chosen; the consolation remains that a part-time president will be less damaging or less of a waste than a full-time president. Assume, conversely, that we have the right person in the right place. In that event we shall have the best of two worlds, namely, a parliamentary system at the height of its performance (interested in avoiding punishment), and a presidential alternative that either stimulates or surrogates parliament's doings. Let me put it thus: that the presidential phase takes care of the 'negatives' of parliamentary government, while the parliamentary phase disposes of the undesirable side-effects of presidentialism. Most political analysts sing high praise of the benefits of alternation in government, of alternative governments. Changing what has to be changed, alternating presidentialism deserves on similar grounds much of the same praise.

Is all of the above difficult – difficult to understand and also difficult to implement? No, absolutely not. The basic idea is – I was saying – that a parliamentary system that performs is rewarded by its continuation, whereas a non-performing parliamentary system is punished by its discontinuance. And that surely is an easily understandable idea. As for the implementation, since intermittent presidentialism combines, in alternation, a parliamentary with a presidential system, whoever buys the idea has only halfway to go. A parliamentary constitution simply needs, in order to be transformed into a system of alternating presidentialism, a presidential addition. Conversely, a presidential constitution requires little more than a parliamentary prefacing. To be sure, in both cases the two parts of the new constitution will require some coordination, while the double nature of the new system allows for improvements in each of its component elements. Still, we are in fact combining elements of mechanisms that are all, by now, well known and abundantly tested. The difficulty that confronts the formula of alternating presidentialism simply is – I submit – the difficulty that confronts any novelty. If we overcome the shock of novelty, all the rest is easy.

NOTES

1. In what follows I draw from Sartori 1992, where the 'alternating presidentialism' proposal is discussed more extensively and in greater detail. A roundtable debate of an earlier outline of my proposal is: G. Amato, A. Barbera, L. Elia, S. Galeotti, A. Manzella, G. Miglio, G. Sartori, 'Parlamentarismo e Presidenzialismo: Dibattito sulla Proposta di Giovanni Sartori', *Il Politico* (LVI), 2, 1991, pp. 201–55.

2. Today Mexico clearly is in transition from a pattern of authoritarian presidentialism sustained by a hegemonic party arrangement (Sartori, 1976, pp. 232–35) to a most unique experiment of presidential democracy whose formula reverses the American one, that is, based on undivided power. So far the transition has basically occurred in the electoral arena, with the electoral reforms enacted in 1989 and 1993. My suggestion in the text relates to the stage at which Mexico will be confronted with executive-level transformations. See also *infra* ch. XI.

3. Strict incompatibility implies that an MP cannot be appointed to the president's cabinet even if he or she resigns. Since the presidentialist phase would be the terminal one of each legislature, leaving parliament carries no loss and would not be, therefore, a deterrent.

10 The Paradox of Governing by Legislating

10.1 INITIATIVE AND VETO

I was saying that the problems of presidentialism are not in the executive arena but in the legislative arena. Thus far, therefore, I have answered only the easy part of the question, How strong should an intermittent president be allowed to be? Its difficult part begins with asking, How can his governing avoid parliamentary obstructionism? More exactly put, How much legislative power does a president need in order to have his legislation passed by parliament?

The beginning is in the notion of governing by legislating.[1] The expression brings to the fore that present-day democracies have settled for governing under the form of law, that is to say, for translating policy decisions into law-like commands. This implies that it is impossible to govern without enacting laws and therefore that parliamentary support is indispensable for governing. The question thus becomes: How can governing and legislating be fused without too much loss on either the executive or the parliamentary sides of the ledger?

Crossing parliament is also a problem, to be sure, for parliamentary governments; but is *the* problem for presidential government.[2] And since the 'crossing difficulty' confronts any kind of presidentialism (thereby including semi-presidentialism), the issue is best addressed, at the outset, in general. In general, then, the legislative-governing powers of presidents comprise a vast array of resources which widely vary from one system to another. Let us organize the overall armory under three main headings, as in the scheme below.

1. Veto powers:
    Pocket veto
    Partial veto
    Package veto

2. Initiative powers:
    Ordinary legislation
    Decree powers
    Emergency powers

3. Referendum and dissolution powers.

Veto powers assume that a parliament can initiate legislation and/or modify the legislative proposals of the executive. If a parliament can only oppose or reject bills of executive origin, then no presidential veto power is needed. However most parliaments do retain some degree of legislative initiative even in presidential systems, and I know of no parliament utterly deprived of modification powers. The veto powers of a president represent, then, his or her defense against parliamentary trespassings, and constitute a typical feature of presidential systems. But there is veto and veto.

The *pocket veto* allows a president to purely and simply refuse to sign a bill. It is a definitive kind of veto, because it cannot be overridden. If a president chooses inaction, that is, not to sign a bill, that bill is as good as dead and there is nothing that anybody can do about it. On the other hand, the pocket veto is an entirely negative power. The *partial veto* – also called, in the United States, line-item veto – is instead very much an active power. The partial veto allows a president to carve into a bill with partial deletions, by cancelling single provisions – and this is an active remaking of that bill. While the partial veto can be overridden, even so it is the veto that presidents need and desire most. For the line-item veto allows them to bust the 'legislative logroll', i.e., the practice of squeezing into a bill – as it travels through the Houses – bundles of patronage riders, of pork-barrel (spending) items, that purely and simply benefit local constituency interests. The American legislative logroll is a scandalous abuse endorsed by custom; and the fact that American presidents have always been denied the partial veto importantly enfeebles or disrupts their legislative initiative.

American presidents are given, in its stead, the *package veto*, the power to reject a bill in its entirety. But the package veto is the least effective veto power. It can be overridden, and presidents are cornered into either giving up the entire package or swallowing a bill with all its logroll.

Veto power is also a function, to be sure, of the ease or difficulty of its overriding by parliamentary action. Most presidential systems follow the American requirement of a two-thirds override majority. But different qualified majorities are conceivable, and lower levels of override are common enough.[3] Clearly, there is no optimal override level. Strongly minoritarian presidents may be insufficiently protected even by a two-thirds override requirement, while majoritarian presidents may have little reason to fear even a bare majority override.

10.2   DECREE POWER

Thus far we have seen what presidents can impede rather than what it is that they can do. Let us move on to their initiative powers. Ordinary initiative powers are by and large the same across all democracies – whether presidential, parliamentary or in-betweens – for they comprise the normal ways of governing by legislating: a president or a government drafts and submits bills to legislative bodies which either approve, reject or amend them in accord with their standard procedures. On this score the major difference between presidential and non-presidential systems is that in the former the area of exclusive authority to introduce legislation is generally more extended than in the latter – with the exception of the budgetary process, which is attributed in any system to executive initiative.

The difference that matters is, however, that presidential systems based on power separation confront a problem – when it comes to governing by legislating – that parliamentary systems based on power sharing do not confront. Shared power 'flows', divided power 'clashes' – or it so would seem. A parliament-created government is, at least in intent and origin, a part of parliament, whereas a president-created government is its counterpart. Of course, if a presidential system enjoys undivided majorities and the support of a disciplined parliamentary party, in that event its governing by legislating poses no problem. But that – we know – is a very rare event. And this explains the salience that *decree powers* generally acquire in most non-parliamentary systems.

Parliamentary governments too are entitled to have recourse to decree laws; but their 'governing by decree' is required to be exceptional, must be justified by urgency, and is submitted to stringent conditions. Instead *decretismo*, governing by decree largely above the heads of parliaments, is endemic and often epidemic in much of Latin America.[4] A current, extreme case of *decretismo* is Brazil. President Sarney issued, during his tenure under the 1988 constitution, 142 emergency decrees, equivalent to one every four days; and in 1990 the Collor government issued 150 decrees, which comes close to one every two working days.[5] *Decretismo* thus becomes – perforce, under the Brazilian circumstances (*supra* 5.4) – the normal instrument of government. Peru's recent vicissitudes are also related to *decretismo*. Upon his election in 1990 President Fujimori did inherit a country plagued by drug traffic, ruined by decades of civil war, by military and demagogic misrule, and in deep economic crisis. Finding his constitution to be unworkable, Fujimori pushed through his radical reforms by presidential decrees; and when the time came for his decrees to be overridden (as they would have been) he illegally dissolved parliament. In these as in other instances *decretismo* is, then, a dysfunctional response of, or to, non-functioning systems.[6]

Presidents are also allowed, as a rule, more extensive emergency powers than their parliamentary counterparts.[7] However, since emergency powers are contemplated by all constitutions – emergencies do occur – I shall not make a particular point of this point. I also propose to deal briefly with dissolution power and with the referendum resource.

In principle, a presidential system based on power separation should not empower the president to dissolve parliament; but attempts to reinforce presidential regimes may give presidents this additional leverage. I have already noted that this infringement of the separation of power principle leaves a presidential system very much as it is; and I do not wish to make a fuss about dissolution power also because its effectiveness resides more in the menace than in the actuation. A parliament does not like to be dissolved, since its members do not particularly enjoy having to fight for their reelection more frequently than needed. So, dissolution is a good deterrent. But when dissolutions do in fact occur, they may turn out to have been useless or even harmful. And the sure thing is that a country that has frequent recourse to early elections is a country in trouble that is not led out of trouble by having 'flash parliaments' that come and go.[8] A last point is this: that while dissolution powers are an anomaly with presidential systems, they are already 'normal' with semi-presidential ones. On the other hand, and as I have previously pointed out, alternating presidentialism does not, and should not, contemplate dissolution.

Finally, referendums. The American presidential system does not contemplate the referendum, but Latin American presidents do employ the referendum instrument as a means for circumventing parliamentary obstruction – either legally (the constitution empowers them to call referendums) or *de facto*. And, in principle, there is no reason why any indirect, representative democracy should refuse a 'direct', referendum-type complement.[9] But the line that separates use and abuse is – in the case of referendums – a very fine line. To wit, the French Fifth Republic has employed the referendum instrument judiciously (and parsimoniously), while Sri Lanka provides to date the best illustration of the extent of abuse that the instrument permits – for the Sri Lankan president is empowered to submit to referendum any bill that parliament rejects. Referendums truly are a double-edged sword that constitution drafters should handle with care.

10.3   CROSSING PARLIAMENT EFFECTIVELY

I now come to the ordinary processes of governing by legislating. The question is: Can we design executive-legislative relationships that dispose of gridlock? This question was very much on the mind of the framers of the constitution of the French Fifth Republic. And their solution was to drastically reduce the legislative role of the National Assembly and to reinforce the hand of the executive via two devices: the 'package vote' (article 44.3), and the *guillotine* (article 49.3).

The package vote permits the government to group articles and amendments selectively (thus excluding the undesired ones), and to require parliament to either accept or reject the package. Most observers, including myself, think well of the package vote. Indeed, if the American president had the line-item veto, he or she would come very close to performing, on this score, like the French executive does. The guillotine is, instead, a much criticized instrument. With the guillotine (French version) the government 'engages its responsibility' on a *projet de loi*, on a bill – and this is like putting a matter to a vote of confidence. However, when the guillotine is invoked all debate ceases, and if parliament does not introduce and vote (under the absolute majority of members requirement) a motion of censure within 24 hours, the bill is considered adopted. This is, to my taste, too crushing.[10] The guillotine is fine in its English version – putting a stop to debates – because governments must have a way of muzzling filibustering, or of blocking pure and simple obstructionism. But the French guillotine goes far too far in opening the doors to abuse.

While the French 1958 constitution does reckon with the gridlock problem, and while there is much to be learned from the experience of the Fifth Republic, nonetheless I am not happy with procedures that basically confront parliament with 'take or leave' injunctions that allow little, if any, room for feedback and mutual interaction. I would thus like to explore *iter legis* procedures that do leave the last word to the executive and yet allow adequate 'voice' to the legislative body. However, this exploration is best confined to the ambit of alternating presidentialism, for this is the context – I believe – that allows for the optimal handling of governing by legislating. Which is not to say, of course, that what I am about to propose applies *only* to alternating presidentialism. Obviously enough, if a suggestion has merit, it can be played back into the overall setting of presidential and semi-presidential systems.

So, how can we unblock presidential *governing* without undermining parliamentary *control?* Within intermittent presidentialism the question specifically addresses the countering of the failings of the parliamentary phase. And the first redressing must be that in the presidential phase the legislative initiative becomes an exclusive prerogative of the executive. But we all know that this is, per se, a blunt sword very much in need of sharpening.

Assume a bicameral parliament. In that event a first resource of the presidentialist president is – I propose – that his bills will not need a double approval, and that he or she is empowered to decide where (to which chamber) each bill will go. There are two reasons for this. One is that it allows a president to circumvent the adverse circumstance of a different majority in the two branches of parliament. The second reason is that it unclogs the legislative process by doubling (to say the least) the processing capacities of a parliament.

Assume now that a presidential bill arrives at the chosen and appropriate parliamentary committee. What is the committee entitled to do? It can of course approve it. But it cannot just reject it, nor approve it in a modified version. The committee that does not like the bill as proposed will return it to the president with amendment proposals that have to be explained by an accompanying document. On this basis the president may do one of three things: he may negotiate the entire bill with the committee, thus securing its committee approval; or he may accept the committee's amendments only in part; or he may wish to stick to his original text. In the latter two cases the bill is now sent to the floor, whose sole option is to approve or reject it. However, and once again, the rejection must be explained and justified by an accompanying document. And it is only if a bill is rejected, and at this stage of the processing, that the president may have recourse to decree legislation. In that event, however, it is the president that is required, in turn, to accompany his decree with a document that explains why he did not accept the changes demanded by the parliamentary committee.

It is apparent that I attribute a great deal of importance to the 'explaining requirement'; and it can be easily guessed that this 'explaining is intended as a countering of pork-barrel politics. The legislative process is, in all democracies, an utterly opaque process. In spite of all the talk about transparency, all the wheelings and dealings that shape legislative outputs remain wrapped in deep haze. They may be denounced, to be sure, by simple speeches of single individuals. But individual voices are easily lost and submerged within the overall chorus of a parliamentary debate. The general idea thus is that the maneuverings hidden between and within the lines of a legislative text must be unveiled and brought to light. The pork barrel, the wire pullers, the hidden interests, all of this must surface and find exposure via formalized adversary procedures.

There is still a loophole in the arrangement that I must now close. A parliament that wants the presidential president to fail still has a weapon: it can waste time by engaging in filibustering and other delaying tactics. So, the president must be empowered, when his bills go to the floor, to guillotine the debate (in the English manner) and to call for an immediate vote. And committees will have to be subjected to stringent time limitations. For example, any bill that is neither approved nor returned to the president with the committee's proposed amendments within a month's time will be considered enacted by omission. However, committees too must be protected, for a president might try to ease the passage of its bills by flooding a committee with an excessive load of legislative proposals. So, parliamentary committees will be entitled to extra time whenever they can make a reasonable case (to some appeal body) that they are being unduly clogged.

As we come to decree legislation, at this stage it is clear that the president's hand must be reinforced – for decrees that are in fact enacted 'against' parliament are not likely to be subsequently converted into law by the same parliament. But why should they? For one, in my machinery decree legislation is a last resort, since the president must first use up and abide by the ordinary procedures. Remember, further, that with intermittent presidentialism the time tenure of the presidential president is particularly short, and this entails that in a matter of two years or so decrees can always be abrogated by the next parliament. But to argue that legislative decrees do not need subsequent parliamentary approval is not to argue that they cannot be overridden. Governing by decree cannot become a free ride, not even under intermittent conditions.

The problem thus becomes to determine override thresholds – and I use the plural because we do need *variable* thresholds. For it makes no sense to preestablish a fixed majority level when popularly elected presidents can be outsiders, or presidents drawn from relatively small parties. Assume that the president's party only obtains a ten percent representation in parliament. In this instance, even a very high override requirement (e.g., even a 75 percent majority) would leave his decree legislation exposed to systematic rejection. Assume now that a president disposes of a comfortable majority in parliament. In this instance a 75 percent override majority becomes a ridiculous obstacle, and even a 51 percent override majority turns out to be an insufficient hurdle for a president that musters, say, a 60 percent parliamentary support. I am thus brought to suggest that what we need is not a fixed override level, but an override *criterion* – such as the following: that in each legislature the override level is the sum total of all the MPs, less the ones that belong to the president's party. Thus a president whose party obtains only 10 percent of the parliamentary seats can be overridden only by a 90 percent majority. Conversely, a president whose party controls 60 percent of the seats can be overridden by a 40 percent vote.[11] The general idea is to make all intermittent presidents equal – regardless of their parliamentary support – in legislative strength. An underlying idea is also to make the president's party 'responsible' for his performance. Here the assumption is that if a president does well, it will pay for his party to be disciplined in supporting him.

10.4 TOWARD SOLVING THE EXECUTIVE–LEGISLATIVE NEXUS

It should be understood that the above is only a first cut – and a tentative one at that. One can surely envisage other ways of handling the executive-legislative nexus. The point to bear in mind is that the problem arises with regard to minoritarian presidents and divided majorities. As long as a president (intermittent or not) enjoys the support of a parliamentary majority, and as long as his or her majority is a real one (i.e., disciplined enough), then he or she only needs, in order to perform efficiently, two resources: the French package vote, and the English guillotine. But what if a president is not backed by a parliamentary majority? Here is the rub, and it is here that we stumble. And it is at this juncture that we must face up, in one way or another, to the problem of decree legislation.

If we pause to think about it, governing by legislating is a very tricky affair, for it brings about 'two governments', two governing powers – for governing by legislating does entail *legislators that govern*. This may sound reassuring; still, two governing powers are a sure recipe for poor governing. The excogitation thus is: let us first allow parliament not to misgovern, and let us otherwise allow a president to govern against parliament. Does that give us a dangerously strong president? No, I have said, because a half-time president can be entrusted with double power, provided that we make sure that its power remains discontinuous. In any event, I would expect a parliament that knows that it cannot win if it chooses to fight the alternating president, to choose not to fight but to negotiate. If so, the last resort of legislation by decree will become unnecessary and will largely remain a dormant deterrent.

Before concluding, let me go back and keep score. It has been my brief that alternating presidentialism is superior to semi-presidentialism and, furthermore, an optimal solution for any non-performing polity. If there is a way of squaring the circle, alternating presidentialism comes close to doing just that. Since its two engines alternate, they cannot work one against the other. But since it does dispose of two engines, it can hardly fail to outperform the single-engine systems. And the gist of my case is this: that both presidentialism and parliamentarism breed within themselves the defects of their merits. However, if the two formulas are called to compete with each other within a mechanism of alternation, the incentives are in place for the merits to be enhanced and the defects to be minimized.

NOTES

1. In this writing I take governing by legislating for granted. In other writings, however, I consider this practice unsound and recommend 'delegification' (see Sartori 1987, pp. 321–28 and especially Sartori 1990, pp. 182–91), both with respect to past legislation and to policy formulations in general.

2. Take Chile and Uruguay, the two Latin American countries that have (overall, and despite everything) the best democratic longevity record of the area. Both have incessantly witnessed executive attempts to bypass congress and/or to increase presidential power. In Chile these attempts go back to the tenure of President Arturo Alessandri (1932–1936), and led to the Allende deflagration in 1973. And the nature of executive power is the centerpiece of the five constitutional changes of Uruguay between 1918–1967.

3. The limiting case is Venezuela, where even a simple majority can end up promulgating a bill over the president's veto (article 173 of the constitution).

4. Technically, *decretismo* includes, and extends to, executive acts that do not have the form of law. But in its non-technical meaning employed here *decretismo* points to the excessive use, and indeed abuse, of legislating by decree.

5. The letter of the 1988 Brazilian constitution does submit its peculiar variety of decree legislation to forceful restraints. The president is authorized to issue *medidas provisorias*, provisional measures, with the force of law only in exceptional, 'urgent' circumstances; and such measures must be subsequently approved by Congress within 30 days. The loophole is that the urgent *medidas* decreed by the president can be re-decreed every month, and that their 'urgency' consists of his saying so.

6. Argentina attests, in addition, to a frequent recourse to enactments by decree for which there is no real need or urgency, and whose constitutional legitimacy is very dubious. Yet this practice goes largely unopposed.

7. Indeed, emergency powers are in some cases extreme and/or abused. For instance, the Colombian constitution (up until 1991) gave presidents the right to declare part or even all the country under a state of siege (in article 121); and Colombia was in fact under a state of siege for 75 percent of the time between 1968 to 1989.

8. My argument does not apply, of course, to the innocuous English practice of 'timing' elections at the best possible moment for the incumbent government.

9. This is not to say that I endorse 'referendum democracy' as a replacement of representative democracy. To this I strongly object in Sartori 1987, pp. 111–20 (chapter 5, sections 7–8). See also, for the analysis of decision-making techniques in general, Sartori 1987, chapter 8.

10. In fairness, it should be noted that French governments have used the guillotine with reluctance, if one is to judge by the fact that between 1959 and 1990 the package vote has been utilized on 236 occasions, whereas the guillotine has been invoked 64 times only.

11. This might appear odd; and yet it seems to me to make a great deal of sense, for a 60 percent majority president does not need to have recourse to decree legislation and should be discouraged from using this shortcut.

11 Problems with Presidential Systems

11.1 REELECTING PRESIDENTS

The most heated debates within most presidential systems currently bear on the tenure of presidents and on their reelectability. I begin, therefore, with these two issues. The fundamental issue remains, however, the support that presidents can expect to obtain in their respective Congresses. The support problem has already been discussed at various points, but one of the indicators that help its assessment is the nature of the party system. I thus bring all these elements together in Table 11.1. The table is not exhaustive; it omits a few countries (Burkine Faso, Dominican Republic) because very small and/ or too unsettled, and South Korea because its presidentialism has only been a 1988–90 interregnum. Note, finally, that the table is strictly confined to 'pure' presidential systems.

How long should presidents be in charge? Chile permits the longest duration in office (eight years, *pro tempore* reduced between 1990–1994 to four in the post-Pinochet transition), followed by Mexico, the Philippines and Nicaragua with six years. Brazil also had a six-year duration, shortened in 1988 to five years. Argentina too is expected to shorten, in 1994, the presidential term from six to four years; a shortening that will be compensated by immediate reelectability. But the table largely speaks for itself. It shows that most presidential countries contemplate a four- to five-year tenure, and that they generally do not permit immediate reelection. However, Bolivia, Brazil, Colombia, Panama, Uruguay and Venezuela permit a second term after an interval (as a rule, the time of the in-between presidency; but Panama and Venezuela only after ten years).

Are duration and reelectability connected? In part, yes. That is to say that there is, or can be, a trade-off between them.

Table 11.1 Characteristics of presidential systems

Country Constitution	Mandate	Reelection	Party System
Argentina			
1853	6 years	No	Twoparty
1994	4 years	Yes	
Bolivia			
1967	4 years	No	Multiparty
Brazil			
1988	5 years	No	Atomized
Colombia			
1886	4 years	No	Twoparty (dubious)
Costa Rica			
1949	4 years	Never	Twoparty
Chile			
1980	8 years (4 years 1990–94)	Never	Multiparty
Ecuador			
1978	5 years	Never	Multiparty
El Salvador			
1983	5 years	Never	Multiparty
Guatemala			
1985	5 years	Never	Multiparty
Honduras			
1982	4 years	Never	Twoparty
Mexico			
1917	6 years	Never	Hegemonic/ Predominant
Nicaragua			
1986	6 years	Yes	Multiparty
Panama			
1972/1983	5 years	No	Multiparty
Paraguay			
1967	5 years	Yes	Multiparty
Peru			
1979	5 years	No	Multiparty
1993	5 years	Yes	Multiparty
Philippines			
1987	6 years	Yes	Twoparty
United States			
1787	4 years (two terms)	Yes	Twoparty
Uruguay			
1967	5 years	No	Twoparty (dubious) Three-party
Venezuela			
1985	5 years	No	Twoparty

Legend: 'No': not consecutively; 'Never': one tenure only.

Not in the case of Mexico, however. Mexico is indeed a very special case, which has long been spoken of as a system that ingeniously manages to retire its dictators every six years. However, since this rule has been firmly adhered to, without a single exception, since 1917, after 75 years the dictum calls for revision. If a dictator is truly a dictator, he cannot be retired. Dictators are such because they 'dictate' the law at their discretion: what is their pleasure *legis habet vigorem*. So, Mexican presidents can be said to have near-dictatorial powers, but cannot be said to be dictators. For dictators stay in office, or reinstate themselves in office, until they are deposed by force or die. In the Mexican case, then, the non-reelectability, ever, of its presidents is the crucial condition that establishes the divide between dictatorship or not. Here there can be no trade-off between duration in office and return to office. But in most instances the Argentinian switch to a shorter duration (from six to four years) in exchange for immediate reelectability appears a reasonable compromise.

The reelectability issue must be confronted, however, on its own merit. The major argument against extending the tenure of presidents is the fear that their reelection may ease their way into becoming dictators. A second argument against reelection is that presidents that can succeed themselves end their term in campaigning for their reelection, while single-term presidents just go ahead with their job. The retorts to this argument are, one, that single-term presidents quickly become enfeebled lame ducks (they cannot promise future protection to their supporters) and, two, that reformist presidents, or presidents worried about who might succeed them, display an undue haste, an undue 'wish *de vouloir conclure*' (as Albert Hirschman has called it). But the fundamental argument in favor of reelectability is that presidents that do well must be rewarded, and that to waste a good president is indeed a serious waste.

There is no denying that each side of the controversy speaks to valid points. This is not an issue that obtains a solution for all seasons. If the fear of a dictatorial relapse is justified, then it beheads the argument, for this is in itself a sufficient reason for denying reelectability (at least, immediate reelectability).[1] On the other hand, if it is a fear arising from past memories rather

than from present-day circumstances, then the winning argument becomes, in my opinion, that any office deprived of
rewards, of 'do well' incentives, is a wrongly conceived office.
True, a reelectable president is tempted to be, in its first tenure,
a demagogic president. But it is equally true that denying reelection is the denying of reward, and that this is a serious flaw.[2]

11.2 TWOPARTY VERSUS MULTIPARTY PRESIDENTIALISM

Let us turn to how presidential systems relate to their
respective party systems. As we have seen (*supra* ch. 6),
'functioning democracy' cannot be confined to twoparty,
majoritarian-based democracies. Multiparty PR-based democracies can also function and be quite functional. But this
argument applies to parliamentary systems and cannot be
extended to presidential systems. Mainwaring is quite right in
pointing out that 'the prevailing wisdom that the number of
parties does not matter much in determining prospects for
stable democracy . . . has overlooked the difference between
parliamentary and presidential systems'. Indeed, 'problems
typical of presidential systems – especially conflict between
the executive and legislature resulting in immobilism – are
exacerbated by multipartism' (Mainwaring, 1993, pp. 222–
23). The evidence well supports this conclusion, for only Chile
has managed to perform since 1933 (with the major interruption of Pinochet's dictatorship, however) as a multiparty
presidentialism. Still, what are the reasons that make presidentialism and multipartism a difficult combination?

In a parliamentary system a prime minister creates his or
her majority by embarking as many parties as needed into a
coalition government. Presidents cannot do that;[3] and if they
are minority presidents they are stuck with their troubles and
must 'shop' for a majority at every twist and turn of their
legislative action. Parliamentarism does not have, then, a
divided majority problem, while presidentialism is haunted
by it. The question thus turns on why 'more parties' make this
problem more intractable.[4] And the reply is that presidential

governments are less likely to stumble into contrary majorities under twoparty than under multiparty situations. Right. But the argument needs underpinning.

A first point to note is that when we say 'two parties' we must make sure that parties are the real units of the play. In my table Colombia and Uruguay are declared twoparty, in part because this is a standard classification, and basically because I could not meaningfully declare them multiparty either. However, both are cases of facade twopartism. In Uruguay parties are not the real actors,[5] and the Colombian twopartism is largely, if not entirely, a manufactured one.[6] The evidence on twoparty presidentialism must be confined, therefore, to five cases: the United States, Venezuela, Argentina, Costa Rica and the Philippines (currently a feeble case).

A second, related point is this: that parties may be the real units in the electoral arena, and yet lose their 'unity' in the parliamentary arena, as parliamentary parties. We are thus brought back to the question whether governability is served better by disciplined or by undisciplined parties. With parliamentary systems the answer clearly is that undisciplined parties are dysfunctional, that they are responsible for the poor showing of the assemblear variety of parliamentarism (*supra* 6.5). With presidentialism, however, the question does not obtain a clear-cut answer. The argument that undisciplined parties facilitate the functioning of presidentialism (see, e.g., Riggs, 1988) cannot be generalized: it is true for divided government, false otherwise. Even so, the point remains that parties matter only if they display a modicum of discipline. Without parliamentary discipline whether parties are two or more does not make much difference. As we have seen with regard to the United States (*supra* 5.2), a majoritarian president that cannot rely on the support of his own party confronts to a significant extent the same problems as a president without majority. In both cases presidents must engage in 'horse trading', in buying votes, one by one, from single members of parliament.

These qualifications do not alter the fact that presidential systems are likely to perform better with twopartism than with multipartism, and that 'the combination of presidentialism and multipartism makes stable democracy difficult to sustain' (Mainwaring, 1993, p. 199). And if this conclusion is accepted, then we must look into how the good combination – twoparty presidentialism – can best be sustained and engineered.

An important help surely comes from 'strong' electoral systems that counter and indeed reduce party fragmentation (*supra* ch. 3).[7] That is the same as saying that it is a mistake to combine presidentialism with PR.[8] As we know a strong, i.e. solidly structured, party system can block, on its own force, party proliferation. Yet the rule of thumb is that if one desires PR then one should not desire a presidential arrangement. Even semi-presidentialism – in spite of its adaptability to divided majorities – is likely to run into more trouble than it needs without a majoritarian electoral system (such as the French double ballot). The formula that can perform under all possible electoral arrangements is the formula of alternating presidentialism. Conversely, the one formula that is most undermined by PR is presidentialism.

11.3 STAGGERED VERSUS SYNCHRONIZED ELECTIONS

The last issue on my agenda is whether presidential and parliamentary elections should be synchronized, or whether they should be left, as is generally the case, asynchronous. The different timing of the two elections is, to be sure, a rebalancing precaution (within an overall mechanism of checks and balances). A rebalancing precaution that runs deep across the entire American system. In the United States the presidential office lasts four years; the House is partially renewed every two years; and the Senate's tenure is six years, with three partial renewals coming every two years. Here everything is minutely piecemealed into asynchrony. Is all this piecemealing useful? What purpose does it serve today?[9]

The basic argument in favor of staggered elections, of partial renovations of Congress and of a different duration of the legislative and presidential tenures is that continuous elections keep the polity in tune with shifts in popular opinion and enhance the responsiveness of politicians. Quite so. The counterargument is that this piecemealing makes the 'majority need' of presidential systems ever more difficult to satisfy. And this is also true. Note that the assumption does not need to be that concurrent elections obtain a coattail effect (often enough they do not). The correct assumption is, however, that a same majority is more easily found at a same time than at different points in time. The choice between concurrent or asynchronous elections hinges, then, on our priorities. If we feel that governability and undivided majorities matter less than responsiveness to popular opinions, then asynchrony is to be preferred. If, instead, we feel that the overriding need of our time is to have performing and responsible governments, then we should opt for synchronized elections. Concurrent elections cannot fabricate undivided majorities that are not potentially in the works; but staggered elections do facilitate divided majority outcomes.

By way of conclusion let me return to the question: Under which conditions presidential systems perform at their best? The answer that I endorse is that twoparty presidentialism is more functional than a multiparty one, and that as ideological differences decline a bipolar,[10] if not a twoparty simplification is favored by: i) the centrality of the presidency, i.e., the effectiveness of presidential power; ii) having parties that perform as principal competitors for the presidency; iii) requiring an absolute majority winner (with a double ballot system); iv) the coinciding of parliamentary and presidential elections. But what if all of this cannot be made to happen? Well, in that event hopeless presidentialism should seriously consider its transformation into either a semi-presidential or an intermittent-presidential system.

NOTES

1. On this consideration, the one-term limit makes sense for Colombia, Ecuador, El Salvador, Guatemala and Honduras, but not, for example, for Costa Rica. At the other extreme, that

Nicaragua, Paraguay and the Philippines should have no limit at all appears unwise.

2. Note, in this connection, that semi-presidential systems (Finland, France, Sri Lanka) do not limit reelectability. And it goes without saying that the problem would not arise with alternating presidentialism.

3. Remember that my argument is structural. Behaviorally presidents can do (have the power to do) as they please. Thus Chile's President Frei (the one elected in 1993) has appointed a broad 'rainbow cabinet' very much in a parliamentary manner. This assumes that appointing a minister of a given party assures a lasting voting loyalty of that party; an assumption that may hold *pro tempore* and for somewhat unique reasons for Chile, but that holds no structural or systemic promise.

4. I must underscore that 'more intractable' is not utterly intractable. The problem created by a multiparty situation is that a president that shops for the votes of party A may lose on this account the votes of party B. Differently put, buying a majority across different parties (a coalitional majority) is much harder than buying the vote of single members within a same party.

5. That is to say that the real political units are, in Uruguay, the *sub-lemas*, the intra-party fractions, of the *lemas* (parties). Furthermore, it is no longer the case that only two *lemas*, the Blanco and Colorado parties, dominate the scene. For a left-oriented coalitional third-party aggregation, the *Fronte Amplio*, has definitely broken in 1971 and subsequently – after the military interval of 1973–1984 – in the 1984 and 1989 elections the traditional bipolar configuration of Uruguayian politics. Thus, even at the largely nominal *lemas* level, Uruguay must be currently classified as a three-party system.

6. In Colombia the Sitges agreement that closed the *Violencia* civil war period established (up intil 1974) that the Liberal and Conservative parties were given, whatever the returns, *paridad*, i.e., an equal number of seats in both chambers. This agreement was then extended up until 1978. Thereafter it was constitutionally established (in Article 120) that the minority party would receive, regardless of turnout, an 'adequate and equitable share' of all appointed government positions. Furthermore, the real electoral units – under the Liberal-Conservative nominal umbrella's – are the *roscas*, i.e.

patronage-based networks organized around individual politicians that present several different party lists. If that is two-partism, then I do not know what two-partism is.

7. Jones (1993, p. 67) finds in the Latin American case 'a strong positive correlation between disproportionality and multipartism for the PR systems' and notes that 'this result is contrary to . . . Giovanni Sartori's hypothesis of an inverse relationship between these two variables'. Jones seemingly misses the crucial caveat that my 'laws' (*supra* 3.3 and 3.4) and, in general, any determination of the influence of electoral systems assumes structured party systems – a condition seldom met in the area. Let it be added that the enormous variance of district magnitudes not only across, but also within most Latin American countries defies the statistical treatment of this variable.

8. Interestingly, Lijphart concurs: 'The Latin American pattern of presidentialism combined with PR legislative elections is a particularly unattractive option' (1991, p. 11). To be sure this is not, with Lijphart, an argument against PR but against presidentialism.

9. Staggered elections also and especially characterize the Upper Houses in Australia, Japan and the Netherlands (one half of the membership is renewed every three years). France renews one third of its Senate every third year; and also the German and Austrian *Bundesrat* are selected in staggered, though irregular, intervals.

10. In the French Fifth Republic this bipolar configuration has been called *quadrille bipolaire*, for it actually consisted, at least until the 1993 election, of two-against-two party aggregations.

12 Problems with Parliamentary Systems

12.1 BICAMERALISM OR NOT

Since all democracies have a parliament, the problems that arise with parliamentary systems are not, in most instances, unique problems, problems that apply only to the parliament-centered polities. They are, however, problems that are more salient, or more thorny, in parliamentary than in other systems.

I begin with the issue that perhaps is most controversial across parliamentary countries, namely, whether they still need bicameral structures. Single-chamber parliaments already exist in nine countries. We additionally have two anomalies, the Norwegian and Icelandic legislatures, which are elected as a single body but then divide themselves into two chambers (in Norway the second chamber is made of one-fourth, and in Iceland of one-third of the members of the elected body). But this is only an internal modification of unicameralism. Thus, in my counting there are eleven unicameral countries: Denmark, Finland, Greece, Israel, Luxembourg, New Zealand, Portugal, Sweden, Turkey, plus Iceland and Norway. We are still left with a majority of democracies that are bicameral.

A first point to note is that wherever the power of the two houses is unequal, the feebler one always is the Upper House (variously called House of Lords, Senate, *Bundesrat*, etc.). Originally the Upper House had, or was intended to have, the last say. But today it is the Lower House (variously called House of Commons, House of Representatives, Chamber of Deputies, *Bundestag*, etc.) that generally prevails. The reasons for this unequal and lesser power of Upper Houses are many. Whenever the Upper House is not of elective extraction (the English House of Lords), or is elected only in part (in the Canadian Senate the prime minister can appoint as many as

183

108 members), then it stands to reason that the Upper House is required to yield to the elected body. A lesser legitimacy may – but also may not – taint the Upper Houses that are elected indirectly (e.g., the French Senate). But Upper Houses are often a subordinate body also when elected directly. Japan's Diet (parliament) is bicameral, both Houses are elected by popular vote and yet its House of Representatives has the upper hand over the House of Councillors, for a law opposed by the latter can be overridden by a two-thirds majority of the former. And there is no instance, in the present-day world, of an Upper House that stands above the Lower one.

There are many varieties of bicameral arrangements. A first distinction, we have just seen, is whether the two Houses are of equal or unequal power. A second distinction is whether the two Houses are similar or dissimilar in nature or composition. With regard to the first distinction, when their strength is very unequal we have feeble (asymmetric) bicameralism, and when it is about equal we have strong (symmetric) bicameralism. Let it also be stipulated that when the two chambers are, in all power respect, on a par, then we have perfect bicameralism. With regard to the second distinction, its explication is as follows: two Houses are similar in nature if they are both elected, and if both represent population and not territory; and are likely to be similar in composition if they are both elected with congruent electoral systems (e.g., both proportional or both majoritarian). Conversely, when these conditions do not obtain, the likely outcome is a differentiated bicameralism.

Intuitively the first variable – *equal–unequal strength* – appears to be the more important one. But the upshot of the second variable is that similarity in nature and composition are conducive to 'similar majorities', whereas dissimilar Houses are conducive to different and conflicting majorities. Upon reflection, then, the degree of *similarity–differentiation* between the two Houses is just as important.

Along these distinctions the problem can be outlined neatly. Bicameralism is upheld against unicameralism on the argument that two Houses are a safety, and that the concentration of all legislative power in just one body is not only dangerous but also unwise: for two eyes are better than one, and prudence wants any decision-making process to be controlled and assisted by brakes.[1] However, if the two Houses are too similar and thus duplicates of one another, they serve no useful garantiste purpose. On the other hand, the more they are made to be dissimilar, the more they may express different majorities that are, in turn, governability killers. The predicament is a real one, and the matter does deserve serious consideration.

It is always nice to have measures for variables. In the case at hand we do. The similarity variable can be measured in many ways, but for our purposes it is the 'outcome measure', so to speak, that matters, i.e., the extent to which a government obtains consonant majorities in both Houses. Here the measure is as simple as a measure can be: for instance, a +20/+50 majority support ratio in the first/second Houses. Conversely, a +20/−50 ratio would indicate a strong dissimilarity, or a similarity failure. Our other variable – equal-unequal power – also lends itself to easy measurement. The indicator is, here, whether the power of the Upper House is only a delaying power (e.g., the British House of Lords) or also a veto power. In the latter case the veto may be i) absolute, that is, without recourse, ii) absolute only in reserved domains, iii) overridable by a qualified majority of the Lower House and, iv) overridable by a simple majority. The latter hardly amounts, however, to a veto power, for one should presume that a bill approved by the Lower House already has a majority backing. The point remains that the overriding majorities vary, and that the higher the override requirement, the more effective the veto power is.

On the other hand, Houses that have an equal power over the legislative process – the case of strong or even perfect bicameralism – are Houses that have in fact a reciprocal veto over one another. There are three such cases in parliamentary systems – Australia, Belgium and Italy – and the United States well exemplifies the case of a strong bicameralism within presidential systems. And here the issue is joined. To be sure, perfect bicameralism is fine so long as the two Houses have a same majority. But what if they do not?

In presidential systems – as in the United States – diverse majorities between the House and the Senate certainly represent a complication; but a complication that presidentialism can handle and is accustomed to handle. But the case is very different, and the problem is a far more severe one, in the context of parliamentary systems. Take what happened in 1975 in Australia when Labor held a majority in the House of Representatives, the Liberal–Country party alliance (a standing one) held a majority in the Senate, and the Senate refused to pass the government's appropriations bills in order to force the Labor government to resign. The deadlock was resolved because Australia is a Commonwealth country with a governor-general that took it upon himself to resolve it (on dubious legal grounds, in my opinion). But without this fortunate and peculiar safety valve Australia would have been confronted, in 1975, with a severe constitutional crisis.

Spelled out, the problem is this: that strong bicameralism – two Houses with equal power – assumes strong similarity, that is, in the final analysis, two Houses with a same (congruent) majority or, at least, whose majorities are not incompatible and mutually hostile. However, similarity in nature and composition (as defined earlier) are facilitating conditions of this outcome, but cannot make it certain. Lijphart argues that 'parliamentarism and strong bicameralism are incompatible only if cabinets tend to be formed on the basis of narrow majorities in the first chamber. If cabinets are grand coalitions they will have no problem. In fact, the obvious solution to the problem of "two mutually hostile majorities" in a strong bicameral legislature is to form an oversized coalition cabinet' (1984a, p. 104). But here Lijphart belittles the problem and – I am afraid – ultimately misses its intractability.

Sure, a grand coalition may be a way out – but almost always a poor one. For minimum-sized coalitions generally are more homogeneous than oversized ones; and this implies that in order to avoid a government-parliament deadlock we may create an intra-governmental deadlock (among mutually dissonant and litigious partners) that is just as unworkable (*supra* 4.2). And then, why would the players in this game want to settle it as Lijphart would like them to do? In the Australian case, one player wanted to oust the other – period – not to enter a grand embrace. It is simply not the case that all political actors can and will accept to govern together. If they relate as cats and dogs, if they truly are ideological enemies, or if they perceive that 'staying out' is in their electoral interest, in all these instances oversized coalition cabinets are neither obvious nor, indeed, possible solutions.

So, what do we do if, with equal bicameralism, we obtain two chambers with dissimilar and mutually hostile majorities? The question has no answer – I submit – other than this: that here we have a problem without solution, or – better – whose solution is only *not to have* strong (symmetric) bicameralism. Two Houses that must assume, in order to function, similar majorities, stand out as a macroscopic instance of ill-conceived constitutionalism. This conclusion, if accepted, eliminates 'bad bicameralism' and allows us to pursue with a clean slate the analysis of good bicameralism.

As we revert to the various possibilities of asymmetric bicameralism, I leave aside the case of an Upper House whose only power is a delaying power. This is an extreme case of feeble, and perhaps excessively feeble, bicameralism whose usefulness must be assessed on *ad hoc* grounds. We still have plenty on which to go with the various levels of veto power that characterize the role and the weight of the Upper Houses. As we have seen, these levels are best measured by how a veto can be overridden. Their veto power is minimal when it can be overridden by the simple majority of the Lower House (as in Austria). At the other extreme the veto power of an Upper House is maximal when it is absolute, that is, when it cannot be overridden (e.g., the Netherlands). Between these extremes we can have mixes of absolute and of overridable veto power (e.g., the German *Bundesrat*) and, of course, different levels of overridability by Lower Houses: qualified majorities of 75 percent, or of 60 percent, or of some sort or other.

While it is obvious that an Upper House is stronger the more it disposes of an absolute veto, and/or the more the overriding of its veto is made impervious, it is interesting to note the strength of some Upper Houses is unrelated to whether they are directly elected or not. For example the Dutch and also the German ones rank quite high in power, and yet are not popularly elected. It is not necessarily the case, then, that the power of an Upper House is a function of its direct democratic investiture and legitimacy.

We are about ready to bring our nets to shore. But let me first wrap the case together. With two variables – how equal is the power, and how similar the composition of a bicameral arrangement – their interplay is, on the one hand, that if the two Houses are too similar, if they are look-alikes, they facilitate governability but serve no useful checking purpose; and, on the other hand, that if they are diversified, they ensure a greater control that also promises gridlock and deadlock. The question thus becomes: how can our two variables be optimally combined? The worst possible combination results from perfect bicameralism. At the other end an extremely feeble bicameralism leaves us at the edge at which bicameralism shades into unicameralism (as in England). Between and across these extremes it should be borne in mind that dissimilar and unequal bicameralism go hand in hand. That is to say that we can afford more dissimilarity the more the two Chambers are unequal and, conversely, that the stronger the bicameralism, the more we must seek and secure similarity.

Now a coda. So far I have dealt with unitary states and have left aside federal states. And federalism confronts *sui generis* problems. With federal structures – and even more with confederal ones – there is little doubt that we need two Houses (the unicameral option is not, here, an option), for we need an Upper House that represents the member states and therefore based on territorial representation. On this requirement it is also apparent that federalism is reinforced by strong bicameralism. Federalism optimally requires, then, two Houses that are equal in force but dissimilar in nature. Are we back, here, to square one? To some extent I am afraid that we are. I say to some extent because presidential systems – as the case of the United States goes to show – empower, or may empower presidents to cope with the problem. But how can it be handled by parliamentary systems?

Two possible answers are illustrated by India and Germany. India handles the problem by sacrificing territorial representation and with feeble bicameralism. India's Upper House, the Raiya Sabba, is elected by the state legislatures but remains conceived as a minor component of a central and strongly centralized federal structure. Germany attests, instead, to a way of truly confronting the issue. The *Bundesrat* is unequal in strength on two counts: it does not have a say in the election or dismissal of the chancellor (this is an exclusive prerogative of the *Bundestag*), and its veto power is absolute only with respect to the legislation that affects the *Länder*. Even so the German *Bundesrat* is a powerful body on account of its being composed by the executives of the member states. All in all, it is Germany, it seems to me, that shows how a federal bicameralism can best be entered in a parliamentary system.

12.2 PARTY DISCIPLINE

Another issue that crucially affects parliamentary systems is the issue of party discipline. Of course party discipline is also a problem within presidential systems – but a lesser one, at least in the sense that here it may cut in two ways. It cuts in one way only, however, in parliament-based systems, for here there is little doubt that 'parliamentary fit' parties (*supra* 5.4) are a vital requirement, and that disciplined party voting is part and parcel of that 'fitness'. The relevance of parties for democratic governance is a point that has been sketchily touched in this work at many points. It should now be confronted in full.

In the present-day world we have both too much and too little party. Somewhere the party is king; somewhere the party is nothing. At one extreme we find the 'octopus party' (as I call it) whose tentacles enter everywhere; at the other extreme we barely manage to locate the womb-party – the party that has yet to be born – or find only the atrophied party.

With regard to too little party let me simply point out that party atrophy leaves the polity with a vacuum, with a void that manifests itself in countless *aggregative failings* along the vertical construction of democracy.[2] When American scholars worry about the withering away of their parties, they are right to worry. And Brazil will never pull its political system together until it rests on the 'atomized party', a state of affairs in which party is little else than a name for politicians that band and disband at whim. Too much party is instead a degeneration, a hypertrophy of party whose extreme manifestation is, I have said, the octopus party and/or (as it is also called) the 'colonizing party'. As the labels suggest, here we have the party that trespasses, then invades and pervades – far beyond the domain of politics – all spheres of society, and thus the truly omnipotent (all powerful) party. Italy has long been – until the ruinous collapse of its *partitocrazia* in 1993 – an extreme instance of a *Parteinstaat* whose parties become a sort of cancer that spreads and corrodes the entire social and economic fabric. But the Austrian *proporz*, Israel, and some countries ennobled as being 'consociational', have equally travelled the path of party colonization to inordinate extents.

Now back to party discipline. As the mapping that I have just drawn clearly implies, party discipline cannot and should not be identified with, or derived from party omnipotence. True, if the party is atrophied or utterly dismembered, then we have a dead seed from which nothing grows. But, remember, the party discipline at issue applies only to the party-in-parliament, and calls only for the parliamentary party to vote in unison. For this we do not need the huge, all-pervading octopus-like party; we only need the *solid party* that belongs to, and brings about, a structured party system[3] and that is solid enough to be in control of the parliamentary voting of its members.

The call for party discipline has an unpleasant ring to it. Many tears are shed over the dire fate of the back-bencher, of the parliamentary *peones* or water-bearers; and much invective is pronounced against the rubber-stamp MP. I sympathize, for I would not myself like any of that. Yet the fact is and remains that a parliamentary government cannot govern without parliamentary support; that support means that the parties that uphold the government can actually deliver the vote of their MPs; and that means, in turn, the capacity to impose uniform voting.

Mind you, voting discipline need not result – as the wording may suggest – from enforcement and punishment. Discipline can be imposed, but can also be spontaneous. Ideological and religious parties – i.e., strong belief-based parties – are, by the same token, cohesive parties, and thus disciplined by their inner cohesion. Indeed, we may distinguish between four varieties of voting along party lines: i) enforced discipline (from party headquarters); ii) spontaneous discipline, i.e., cohesion; iii) rational discipline resulting from self-interest (upholding one's own single-party government);[4] iv) discipline by contagion or feedback, resulting from the need of holding together against other disciplined parties.

To be sure, these are analytic distinctions. In most parliaments the ingredients of enforcement, cohesion, self-interest and contagion can all be found to exist and to mix. In a cabinet system discipline is 'rational' but also, if the need arises, enforced; in multiparty parliaments with a large ideological spread (polarized party systems) some parties are cohesive, and other parties are disciplined instead by feedback, because an undisciplined army cannot hold against a disciplined one; and so forth. Yet, the word discipline – with its undertone of something that is imposed – is appropriate for all the varieties, yes, of 'discipline'. When voting along party lines comes 'naturally' or 'rationally', this is all for the better. Nonetheless there is a point at which the party – its secretary and its directorate – must have the capability of obtaining discipline by enforcement. Note that the more the party has this power, the less it actually needs to use it. We should not be mislead, on this score, by appearances of 'spontaneous obedience'. One's conforming to orders comes easy and cheap when the alternative – non-conforming – may carry heavy penalties.

I was saying earlier that party discipline presupposes the solid party. But which solidity is specifically involved in this matter? The question turns on the conditions that put party above member, that is to say, that enable the party to control and condition the behavior of its members. Since we are dealing here with individuals that run for political office, the problem boils down to whether an MP can elect itself by itself, or whether his or her election crucially hinges on party backing. In the first case the party is not in control; in the second we have the 'solid party' that is. And I would say that a party can discipline its members if either one of these conditions obtain: i) the existence of a party organization all the way down to the constituency level – as distinct from the candidate's own – without which a candidate cannot make it; ii) that political money mainly flows through party (or sub-party) channels, and does not go directly to the candidate. Conversely put, an MP that wins his or her election with its own machine and its own money is not party controlled.

There is, however, another face or side to the solid party. The solid party must not only deliver the votes it controls, but must also be a *stable party* in the sense of being a party that roughly holds on to its numbers (the number of its parliamentary members) across each legislature. For there is little point in having a disciplined vote if thereafter the 'voting units' easily and frequently change. We thus come to the problem of defection and of party splits. In stable Western democracies this problem is easily overlooked. But the end of the Japanese predominant party system was brought about, in 1993, by the splitting of the LDP, of its predominant party. And India has long been plagued by amorphous and typically unstable parties. Indeed, members of India's parliament have developed, over the decades, quite an expertise in splittings and switchings. India has also developed, however, countermeasures. In the House of the People (Lok Sabba) an MP who defects loses its seat. But this only deters single defections, and a way of circumventing the punishment is to declare a party split. So, when is a split a split? In India only when a party is left by one-third of its members.[5]

Within structured party systems punishing a party defector with the loss of his or her seat appears to be an unnecessary and excessive punishment. However, as even structured party systems are currently undergoing destructuring, party switchings should not be eased nor rewarded. For instance, while MPs are allowed to leave the party that elected them, they are not allowed to join another party: they can only join a pool of unaffiliated members (the independent parliamentary group). To be sure, an 'independent' MP can always behave like a 'dependent' one – but at his or her own choosing, not because of any imposed discipline, and thus without a discipline alibi to display at election time. On the other hand, the impediments and penalties devised in India surely hold a lesson for a country like Brazil and for the fluid parties that mark the beginnings of competitive politics in post-communist countries.

It should be understood that all of the above is not intended to extol the party 'dependence' of MPs, but only to underscore that if this is an evil, it is a necessary one. It is nice to celebrate the Burkeian independent representative that answers only to his judgement, or otherwise its very opposite, the constituency-dependent one. But the advocates of these niceties forget to tell us how an atomized parliament of independent members or, alternatively, a parliament fragmented into hundreds of constituency-serving delegates, can be, in any meaningful sense, a 'working parliament'. On the other hand it should also be understood that party voting discipline is not, per se, a negation of intra-party democracy. In an appropriately conceived decision-making process, the party line on the issues that come to parliament should first be discussed and deliberated with democratic openness within the party structure. For instance, Japan goes very far – if at the cost of an excessive slowing down – in seeking a consensus-based unity of action also in politics. The point only is, then, that when the intra-party democratic procedures have been exhausted, at that moment the minority opinion(s) has to yield and the party must speak, in voting, with one voice. Putting all in a nutshell, parliament-dependent government implies party-supported government; a support that in turn requires voting discipline along party lines.

I stop here. There are, to be sure, many other problems that typically arise within the context of parliamentary systems. A major one bears on the stability and effectiveness of governments; but this problem has been discussed earlier (*supra* 6.6). An equally serious problem of parliamentarism is coalition government with respect to the homogeneity-heterogeneity of multiparty cabinets; but, again, this is an issue analyzed earlier (*supra* 4.2). We then have problems that are of equal salience in both parliamentary and presidential systems – for instance, the problem of executive–legislative relationships, of how legislation 'crosses' parliament. However, since this is a common problem, it has been covered in chapters 9 and 10. Here, then, I have been dealing with leftovers. And there always are leftovers that are left out.

NOTES

1. Another argument is that unicameralism is suited to small states and bicameralism to large states. There is, to be sure, some intuitive plausibility to this argument at its extremes. I can see, for example, that Iceland and Luxembourg (with a population, respectively, of 250,000 and 370,000) have little use for two chambers, while India can be said to need them. But Ireland, Austria and Belgium are relatively small countries. Should they too dismiss their second chambers on account of their size? Apart from the size point, I certainly do not concur with the generalized view (e.g., Gordon Smith, 1976, p. 166) that Upper Houses are obsolete and 'anachronistic' bodies.

2. For the distinction between horizontal and vertical democracy see Sartori, 1987, esp. ch. 6. The notion of aggregative failing draws, instead, on the standard distinction of Gabriel Almond between the articulation and the aggregation of interests.

3. Party system solidification, and thereby the coming about of the solid parliamentary party, has been well studied with reference to the European latecomers to democracy, especially Spain, Portugal, and Greece. See Morlino (1980), and Liebert and Cotta eds. (1990). This literature implicitly provides insights on how Eastern Europe and former Soviet countries may best seek party solidification.

4. This especially applies to two-party and predominant party systems (*supra* 6.3 and 6.4) but also, more generally, to premiership systems. With any single party government the cost of undiscipline is to oust one's own party from government.

5. Since Indians have become very sophisticated in these maneu-
    verings, the game does not end here. When a party expels some
    of its members the expelled do not lose their seats, but the party
    reduces its overall size. Hence, fewer members have to split in
    order to qualify under the one-third requirement. But while no
    obstacle is insuperable, raising obstacles helps.

13 Constitutional Engineering

It serves no useful purpose, in my opinion, to refer 'constitutionalism' all the way back to the Greeks and the Romans. The Greek term for what we call constitution was *politeía* (which is also translated 'republic'), and the Latin *constitutio* had nothing to do with what we call constitution (Sartori, 1962). As we reach the middle of the seventeenth century, during Cromwell's protectorate the notion of constitution had yet to appear. The time of Cromwell was the time in which the English especially engaged in what we conceive as constitution-drafting. Yet, the documents of the time were called covenants, instruments, agreements, and fundamental law – never 'constitution'. The term constitution and with it the notion of 'constitutionalism' is, then, an eighteenth century coinage, and gained general acceptance in our meaning of the concept in the wake of the American constitution-making experience.

The first written constitutions of modern times – the constitutions of Virginia, Maryland and Pennsylvania – were enacted in 1776. They included a Bill of Rights, but their main body consisted in a 'plan' or 'frame' of government. And the Philadelphia convention of 1787 established only a frame of government, dealt only with the main body. At Philadelphia both Madison and Hamilton opposed the inclusion of a bill of rights in the constitution on the argument that rights were not protected by declarations but by the very structures of constitutional government. A bill of rights was thus proposed by the first Congress two years later, in 1789, and was entered in the federal constitution of the United States under the form of its first ten amendments in 1791.

Is a constitution without a bill of rights an incomplete constitution? I would agree with Madison and Hamilton that declarations of rights are not a necessary condition of constitutions. But in vital matters some redundancy does not hurt, and under the impetus of the various French declarations of the rights of men and citizens, bills of rights have usefully won their way into nineteenth- and twentieth-century constitutions. However, the early declarations of rights were true complements to, and reinforcements of the overall 'protective design' of constitutionalism in that their message basically asserted 'thou shall not': that there were things that governments could *not* do.[1] As bills of rights were expanded in our century to include 'affirmative rights', social and material rights such as rights to education, to employment, to health care, and so forth, their nature and role has taken an entirely new twist. Today 'rights' are more important than ever, but one may doubt whether their transformation in material entitlements still belongs to the constitutional fabric.

I would put it thus: that a constitution without a declaration of rights still is a constitution, whereas a constitution whose core and centerpiece is not a frame of government is not a constitution. To be sure (it should go without saying) constitutions are a plan or frame of 'free government'. As a manner of speech we have fallen into the careless habit of calling any and all state forms constitutions. As a matter of correct understanding it should be understood, however, that for constitutionalism – and most definitely in my argument – constitutions are only the state forms in which (as Rousseau said) we are free because we are governed by laws and not by other men. Robert Filmer, a royalist defender of Charles I still held, in 1648, that 'every power of making laws must be arbitrary: for to make a law according to law is a *contradictio in adiecto*'. Well, constitutionalism represents the defeat of that alleged contradiction. And Madison magnificently compounded the problem in *The Federalist*, no. 51: 'In framing a government which is to be administered by men over men . . . you must first enable the government to control the governed; and in the next place obligate it to control itself'. So, constitutions are, first and above all, instruments of government which limit, restrain and allow for the control of the exercise of political power. And I insist on this *telos*, on this quintessential intent of constitutionalism, because present day constitution-makers pay too little heed, if any, to the very reason for being of constitutions.

Of the 170 or so written documents called constitutions in today's world, more than half have been written since 1974. Whether these constitutions apply to new states or rewrite previous constitutions,[2] in all cases at every writing they tend to become longer and more bulky. The American constitution of 1787–1791 runs, in most textbooks, some fifteen to twenty pages and consists of seven Articles subdivided into a total of 21 Sections (plus the first ten Amendments). The nineteenth-century European constitutions were somewhat longer, but moderately so. Constitutional graphomania begins, by and large, after World War Two. Japan's constitution of 1947 was about twice as long as the Meiji constitution that preceded it, and yet was reasonably brief as contemporary constitutions go: it consisted of a Preamble, 11 Chapters, and 103 Articles. The quantum leap occurred in 1950 with India's constitution, which carried 395 Articles, plus a number of detailed schedules. But it is the Brazilian constitution of 1988 that possibly beats all records: it is a *novela* of the size of a telephone directory, with 245 firm Articles, plus 200 transitional items. It is a constitution packed not only with trivial details but also with quasi-suicidal provisions and unaffordable promises.[3] Peru's constitutions are equally hair-raising. The one of 1979 displays 307 Articles, many of which are sub-itemized at great length.[4]

I shall not go as far as to state that the greater the length of a constitution, the lesser its constitutional merit. Still, I most definitely do not think that constitutions should provide what ordinary legislation is required to provide; and I do feel that the more we establish all-regulating and all-promising constitutions, the more we prompt their infringement and a country's debacle. Be that as it may, in this work my focus has only been on the main body of constitutionalism and specifically on the efficient 'framing' of the polity – under the twin assumptions that most recent constitutions are poor instruments of government, and that this is the failing that most needs to be addressed.

Constitutions have gone astray also because the theory of constitutions and constitutionalism have gone astray. Over the last decades we have been told that constitutions do not matter, that free societies result from societal pluralism far more than from constitutional contrivance. That was the behavioral absurdity. Fortunately behavioralists are now 'rediscovering the state', admit that it has an organizational base, and that it is wrong to conceive structures, and constitutional structures in particular, as mere 'role patterns'. But other absurdities subsist and may even be gaining momentum – especially the notion that constitutions are justice-seeking instruments.

This view is argued by Jon Elster as follows: that 'it is impossible to predict with certainty or even quantified probability the consequences of a major constitutional change', and therefore that constitutional change can be justified only on grounds of justice, not of consequential arguments (1988, p. 304 and 303–23 *passim*). I couldn't disagree more. To begin with, if one takes a non-consequentialist view, one must be consistent across the board. If the consequences of institutional structures are impossible to predict, then the same darkness – and I would say an even greater one – should apply to reforms dictated by justice. And given that justice and (in Elster's case) 'arguments from equality' represent a magnitude of undertaking that exceeds hundredfold the normal, earth to earth, intents of constitutions, the non-consequentialist has no way of showing, on his own premises, that he is not seeking a paradise that will eventually turn into an inferno (as he should know not on predictive grounds, but *ex post*, because it has recently happened under his nose). The preliminary caveat thus is that the non-consequentialist is not entitled to seek or propose anything. The practical implication of the inability of predicting is the inability of reforming.

The above is *arguendo*, for the sake of the argument. But what is the *bien fondé*, the validity, of Elster's case against constitutional predictability? His case is built on two premises, namely, that on the one hand we cannot predict 'the global net long-term equilibrium effects of major institutional changes', while on the other hand 'piecemeal social engineering . . . is of little help as a remedy to this theoretical deficit' (1988, pp. 308–9).

Maybe. But does this reasoning have any bearing at all on what constitutions do and are required to do? I think not.

To descend from abstract pomposities to a concrete constitutional provision, let me pick up for illustration Article 40 of the 1958 French constitution, which reads: 'the proposals and amendments initiated by members of parliament cannot be taken into consideration when their adoption would either reduce the fiscal revenue or impose a financial burden on the budget'. The predicted intent of that brief (but highly consequential) provision was to block parliamentary budget busting; and the prediction has obviously turned out to be entirely correct. To be sure, under that provision a country can still spend, tax and indebt itself; but under that provision governments can no longer play the blame game and lay the blame of financial demagoguery on their parliaments; now we now for sure, from the constitution itself, that it is the government, and the government only, that is responsible for the public debt; and that was, again, the intent. So, we have here a predicted effect that was predictable *ex ante*, that was, we know *ex post*, well predicted, and that has obviously nothing to do with 'global net long term equilibrium effects'.

Leaving minutiae aside, across this work I have been predicting the effects of electoral systems, and I have long engaged in 'condition analysis', that is, in specifying the conditions under which specific constitutional reforms – including major ones – are likely to 'cause' (or not) the intended effects. All of that should be, for Elster, impermissible and/or foolhardy. But I think, instead, that Elster's case against institutional consequentialism and predictability is totally blown out of proportion and quite mistaken. And the point is that throughout his argument Elster seemingly confuses form with content, procedure with what is processed.[5]

Constitutions are pathways. They do not establish that the citizens of, say, Elstonia must all march in unison to the heavenly city of, say, Justopolis. Constitutions simply say: if Elster wants you to reach Justopolis, then Elster must 'follow the path', beginning with winning a majority for his cause via free elections. Assume now that Elster gets through all the constitutional routes, checks and hurdles that he is required to pass. And assume, next, that his march to Justopolis does not get him there. Would that be a constitutional predictive failure? Of course not; it would be a policy failure caused by Elster's predictive errors.

Playfulness aside, constitutions are 'forms' that structure and discipline the state's decision-making processes. Constitutions establish *how* norms are to be created; they do not, and should not, decide *what* is to be established by the norms. That is to say that constitutions are, first and above all, *procedures* intent upon ensuring a controlled exercise of power. Therefore, and conversely, constitutions are, and must be, *content-neutral*. A constitution that takes it upon itself to establish policies, i.e., policy contents, preempts the popular will and tramples upon the policy-making bodies (parliaments and governments) to which the policy decisions are constitutionally entrusted.

We must beware, therefore, of 'aspirational constitutions'. Just as we have had, with disastrous consequences, target economies (the Soviet-type, centrally planned economy), we are currently nurturing 'target constitutions' which are just as likely to be disaster-producing. Aspirational constitutions are, in the end, a deviation and an overload of constitutional capacities that results, in turn, in their failure to function. If constitution-makers cannot resist the temptation of displaying the panoply of their noble intentions, these should be confined to a 'programmatic' Preamble of intents and entitlements.[6] Thereafter, however, constitution-drafters should seriously attend to what they are seriously required to do, namely, the establishing of a frame of government that meets, inter alia, the requirements of governing.

It is time to bring this work to a close, and it is fitting to close it with reference to its title, to my saying 'constitutional engineering'. The eighteenth- and nineteenth-century constitution-makers well understood the *telos*, the end purpose, of constitutionalism and their constitutions were crafted (*pace* Elster) with a 'consequentialist focus' on how they would and should work. These constitution-makers thus were 'natural' engineers. But legal positivism and analytical jurisprudence have brought up – especially in Europe and Latin America –

generations of constitutional lawyers whose only concern and training was in the deductive consistency of a legal universe. To them a constitution is just a well connected system of injunctions, of commands and prohibitions; and any other consideration is extra-juridical, a concern of no concern. The truth of the matter is, however, that no organization can function on injunctions alone, without the complement of an appropriate structure of incentives, and that this is eminently true for the house of power and the 'organizing of power'; for here we come to the point at which injunctions become largely self-addressed (its receivers are also its issuers), and therefore to the point at which orders and prohibitions are more easily bent or ignored. Which hammers the point that the organization of the state requires more than any other organization to be kept on course by a structure of rewards and punishments, of 'good' inducements and 'scary' deterrents.

I conclude, then, on this note: that the more we lose the notion that constitutions must be incentive-monitored and incentive-sustained, the more it must be underscored that the crafting of constitutions is an engineering-like task. A century ago to say constitutional engineering would have been pleonastic; but to say so today is to remind us of something that we have been forgetting.

pleonastic

NOTES

1. This is not to deny that any right is, in principle, affirmative. The right of free speech entitles one to speak; the right of free association entitles one to create and sustain associations, etc. Even so 'formal' rights are very different from 'material' entitlements In the first case the state must refrain from action; in the second it is called upon to act. See Sartori, 1993, pp. 321–4.

2. A rewriting that has been incessant in Latin America, where since their independence some twenty countries have promulgated some 260 constitutions. Brazil has had eight; Venezuela twenty-five. It is a long list.

3. ' "The 1988 constitution promised heaven on earth but ended up hurting the poor," the welfare minister Antonio Britto is fond of saying. He should know. Not only did he help to write it but it is his ministry, notably, that has to pay for the results: ballooning pensions, hospital bills and social security benefits for more than 100 million in a country which, at least officially, has only 23 million wage earners.' (Quoted from *The Economist*, October 9, 1993, p. 45).

4. To cite but one example out of hundreds, Article 233 on the 'guaranties of the administration of justice' of Peru's 1979 constitution is itemized into 19 specifications, one of these being that any person has the right to use his own language and therefore that 'if necessary the judge or the court will secure the presence of an interpreter'. Shouldn't this be a matter of ordinary legislation or, better still, of administrative ruling?

5. Indeed, Elster believes that his argument is about institutional change whereas, in fact, it is only about policy contents. He advocates the overhauling of property rights, equality of treatment and of influence, and economic democracy. The English parliament could decide to do all of that (and still more) without anybody claiming that the English constitution has been changed by a hair's breadth.

6. I make reference here to the Italian legal distinction between 'programmatic' and 'imperative' norms. The former, the *norme programmatiche* are, so to speak, tendency norms, rules that are to be applied only when, and to the extent that, they are applicable. It is only the latter, the *norme precettive*, that have instead the full force of constitutional commands. It is thus understood that when the Italian constitution asserts, e.g., that 'The Republic protects the landscape' this is a programmatic norm that does not entitle millions of Italians to sue the state on millions of occasions for its landscape neglect.

Bibliography

Bogdanor, Vernon, and David Butler, eds (1983), *Democracy and Elections* (Cambridge: Cambridge University Press).

Daalder, Hans (1971), 'Cabinet and Party Systems in Ten Smaller European Democracies', *Acta Politica*, pp. 282–303.

Diamond, L., J. Linz and S. M. Lipset, eds (1989), *Democracy in Developing Countries* (Boulder, Co.: Lynne Rienner (in 4 vols).

Di Palma, Giuseppe (1990), *To Craft Democracies: An Essay on Democratic Transitions* (Berkeley: University of California Press).

Duverger, M. *et al.* (1950), *L'Influence des Systèmes Electoraux sur la Vie Politique* (Paris, Colin).

Duverger, Maurice (1954, 2nd edition), *Les Partis Politiques* (Paris: Colin). The first edition appeared in 1951.

—— (1980), 'A New Political System Model: Semi-Presidential Government', in *European Journal of Political Research*, (8) 2, pp. 165–87.

Eckstein, Harry, and D. E. Apter, eds (1963), *Comparative Politics: A Reader* (New York: Free Press).

Farquharson, R. (1969), *Theory of Voting* (New Haven: Yale University Press).

Finer, S. E., ed. (1975), *Adversary Politics and Electoral Reform* (London: Wigram).

Fisichella, Domenico (1982; 2nd edition 1992), *Elezioni e Democrazia* (Bologna: Il Mulino).

Grofman, Bernard, and Arend Lijphart, eds (1986), *Electoral Laws and their Political Consequences* (New York: Agathon Press).

Grumm, John C. (1958), 'Theories of Electoral Systems', *Midwest Journal of Political Science*, November.

Jones, Charles O. (1990), 'The Separated Presidency', in Anthony King, ed., cit., ch. 1.

Jones, P. Mark (1993), 'The Political Consequences of Electoral Laws in Latin America and the Caribbean', *Electoral Studies* (12) 1, March, pp. 59–75.

Katz, Richard S. (1980), *A Theory of Parties and Electoral Systems* (Baltimore: Johns Hopkins Press).

Key, V. O. (1949), *Southern Politics* (New York: Knopf).

—— (1956), *American State Politics* (New York: Knopf).

—— (1964, 5th edition), *Politics, Parties and Pressure Groups* (New York: Crowell).

King, Anthony, ed. (1990, 2nd version), *The New American Political System* (Washington, DC: American Enterprise Institute).

Lakeman, E., and Lambert, J. D. (1955), *Voting in Democracies* (London: Faber & Faber).

Liebert, Ulrike, and Maurizio Cotta, eds (1990), *Parliament and Democratic Consolidation in Southern Europe* (London, Pinter).

Lijphart, Arend (1968a), 'Typologies of Democratic Systems', in *Comparative Political Studies*, I.1, pp. 3–44.

—— (1968b), *The Politics of Accommodation: Pluralism and Democracy in the Netherlands* (Berkelely: University of California Press).

—— (1977), *Democracy in Plural Societies: A Comparative Exploration* (New Haven: Yale University Press).

—— (1984a), *Democracies: Patterns of Majoritarian and Consensus Government in Twenty-One Countries* (New Haven: Yale University Press).

—— and B. Grofman, eds (1984b), *Choosing an Electoral System* (New York: Praeger).

—— (1985), 'The Field of Electoral Systems Research: A Critical Survey', in *Electoral Studies* (4) 1, pp. 3–14.

—— (1986), 'Degrees of Proportionality in Proportional Representation Formulas', in Grofman and Lijphart, eds, cit., ch. 10.

Linz, Juan (1990), 'The Perils of Presidentialism', in *Journal of Democracy*, (I),1, Winter 1990, pp. 51–69. The essay is the printed, abridged version of a widely-circulated 1985 paper.

—— and Arturo Valenzuela, eds (1994), *The Failure of Presidential Democracy* (Baltimore: Johns Hopkins University Press).

—— and Alfred Stepan, eds (1978), *The Breakdown of Democratic Regimes* (Baltimore: Johns Hopkins University Press).

Lipset, S. M., and Stein Rokkan, eds (1967), *Party Systems and Voter Alignments* (Glencoe: Free Press).

—— and William Schneider (1983), *The Confidence Gap*, New York: Free Press.

Mackenzie, W. J. M. (1958), *Free Elections* (London: George Allen & Unwin).

Mainwaring, Scott (1990), 'Presidentialism in Latin America', in *Latin American Research Review* (25).

—— (1991), 'Politicians, Parties and Electoral Systems: Brazil in Comparative Perspective', in *Comparative Politics*, October, pp. 21–43.

—— (1993) 'Presidentialism, Multipartism and Democracy: The Difficult Combination', in *Comparative Political Studies*, (26), 2, July, pp. 198–228.

—— and T. R. Scully, eds (1994), *Building Democratic Institutions: Parties and Party Systems across Latin America* (Stanford: Stanford University Press).

Mayhew, David R. (1991), *Divided We Govern: 1946–1990* (New Haven: Yale University Press).

Morlino, Leonardo (1980), *Come Cambiano i Regimi Politici* (Milano: Angeli).

Neustadt, R. E. (1960), *Presidential Power* (New York: Wiley).

Nohlen, Dieter (1978), *Wahlsysteme der Welt* (München: Piper). This is the best and most complete description of electoral systems worldwide.

—— (1984a), 'Two Incompatible Principles of Representation', in Lijphart and Grofman, eds, cit., ch. 8.

—— (1984b), 'Changes and Choices in Electoral Systems', in Lijphart and Grofman, eds, cit., ch. 21.

—— ed. (1993), *Elecciones y Sistemas de Partidos en America Latina* (San José, Costa Rica: IIDH [Instituto InterAmericano Derechos Humanos]).

Nordlinger, Eric (1972), *Conflict Regulation in Divided Societies* (Cambridge, Mass.: Harvard Studies in International Affairs).

Polsby, Nelson W. (1993), 'Does Congress Work?', in *Bulletin* of the American Academy of Arts and Sciences, (XLVI), No. 8, May.

Rae, Douglas (1971, 2nd edition), *The Political Consequences of Electoral Laws* (New Haven: Yale University Press). The first edition is of 1967.

Riggs, Fred W. (1993), 'Fragility of the Third World Regimes', in *International Social Science Journal*, (136), May, pp. 198–243.

—— (1988), 'The Survival of Presidentialism in America: Para-Constitutional Practices', in *International Political Science Review*, (9), pp. 247–78.

Riker, W. H. (1982), 'Two-Party Systems and Duverger's Law', in *American Political Science Review*, December, pp. 153–66.

Rose, Richard (1983), 'Elections and Electoral Systems: Choices and Alternatives', in Bogdanor and Butler, eds, cit., pp. 20–45.

—— (1984), 'Electoral Systems: A Question of Degree or of Principle?', in Lijphart and Grofman, eds, cit., pp. 73–81.

Sani, Giacomo, and Giovanni Sartori (1983), 'Polarization, Fragmentation and Competition in Western Democracies', in Hans

Daalder and Peter Mair, eds, *Western European Party Systems* (Beverly Hills: Sage), cit., pp. 307–40.

Sartori, Giovanni (1968a), 'Representational Systems', in *International Encyclopedia of the Social Sciences*, vol. XIII (New York: Macmillan & Free Press), pp. 465–74.

—— (1968b), 'Political Development and Political Engineering', *Public Policy*, volume XVII (Cambridge, Mass., Harvard University Press).

—— (1976), *Parties and Party Systems: A Framework for Analysis* (New York: Cambridge University Press). Translations: Alianza Editorial, Madrid, 1980 (2nd edition 1993); Waseda University Press, Tokyo 1980; Brasilia University Press, Brasilia 1982.

—— (1979), *La Politica: Logica e Metodo in Scienze Sociali* (Milano: SugarCo). Translations: Brasilia University Press, Brasilia, 1982; Fondo de Cultura, Mexico City, 1984 (1987).

—— (1984a), 'Le Leggi sulla Influenza dei Sistemi Elettorali', in *Rivista Italiana di Scienza Politica*, 1, (April), pp. 3–44.

—— (1984b), 'Guidelines for Concept Analysis', in Sartori ed., *Social Science Concepts: A Systematic Analysis* (Beverly Hills: Sage).

—— (1986), 'The Influence of Electoral Systems: Faulty Laws or Faulty Method?', in Grofman, Lijphart, eds, cit., ch. 2.

—— (1987) *The Theory of Democracy Revisited* (Chatham, NJ: Chatham House). Translations: Alianza Editorial, Madrid, 1988; Editorial Losada, Buenos Aires, 1990; Wissenschaftliche Buchgesellschaft, Darmstadt, 1992; Center for the Study of Democracy, Sophia, 1992; Archa Publishing House, Bratislava, 1993; Turkish Political Science Association, Ankara, 1993; Editora Atica, Sao Paulo, 1994; Polish Scientific Publishers, Warsaw, 1994; Ditura Publishers, Tirana, 1944; Progress Publishers, Moscow, 1994.

—— (1989), 'Video-Power', in *Government and Opposition*, Winter, pp. 39–53.

—— (1990, 2nd edition), *Elementi di Teoria Politica* (Bologna: Il Mulino). Translated (1992), Alianza Editorial, Madrid.

—— (1992), *Seconda Repubblica? Sì, Ma Bene* (Milano: Rizzoli).

—— (1993), *Democrazia: Cosa È* (Milano: Rizzoli). Translated in Mexico and Columbia.

Seferiades, Seraphim (1986), 'Polarization and Nonproportionality: The Greek Party System in the Postwar Era', in *Comparative Politics*, October, pp. 69–93.

Shugart, M.S. and J.M. Carey (1992), *Presidents and Assemblies: Constitutional Design and Electoral Dynamics* (New York: Cambridge University Press).

Smith, Gordon (1976, 2nd edition), *Politics in Western Europe: A Comparative Analysis* (London: Heinemann).

Sprinzak, Ehud and Larry Diamond, eds (1993), *Israeli Democracy under Stress* (Boulder: Lynne Rienner).

Strom, Kare (1990), *Minority Government and Majority Rule* (Cambridge: Cambridge University Press).

Sundquist, James L. (1992, revised edition), *Constitutional Reform and Effective Government* (Washington, DC: The Brookings Institution).

Taagepera, Rein and Matthew Soberg Shugart (1989), *Seats and Votes: The Effects and Determinants of Electoral Systems* (New Haven: Yale University Press).

Valenzuela, Arturo (1985), 'Origins and Characteristics of the Chilean Party System: A Proposal for a Parliamentary Form of Government', The Wilson Center, Working Paper No. 164.

—— (1987), 'Party Politics and the Failure of Presidentialism in Chile', paper, Chicago APSA conference.

Vanhanen, Tatu (1990), *The Process of Democratization: A Comparative Study of 147 States, 1980–1988* (New York: Crane Russak).

Index